First World War
and Army of Occupation
War Diary
France, Belgium and Germany

40 DIVISION
Headquarters, Branches and Services
Commander Royal Engineers
3 June 1916 - 28 February 1919

WO95/2597/2

The Naval & Military Press Ltd
www.nmarchive.com
Published in association with The National Archives

Published by

The Naval & Military Press Ltd

Unit 10 Ridgewood Industrial Park,

Uckfield, East Sussex,

TN22 5QE England

Tel: +44 (0) 1825 749494

www.naval-military-press.com

www.nmarchive.com

This diary has been reprinted in facsimile from the original. Any imperfections are inevitably reproduced and the quality may fall short of modern type and cartographic standards.

Contents

Document type	Place/Title	Date From	Date To
Heading	WO95/2597/2		
Heading	War Diary of Headquarters 40th Divisional Engineers October 1918 Volume 29		
Heading	War Diary of Headquarters 40th Divisional Engineers From 3rd June 1916 To 30th June 1916 Volume 1		
War Diary	Southampton	03/06/1916	03/06/1916
War Diary	Havre	04/06/1916	05/06/1916
War Diary	Abbeville	06/06/1916	06/06/1916
War Diary	Lillers	06/06/1916	06/06/1916
War Diary	Ligny Lez Aire	06/06/1916	19/06/1916
War Diary	Bruay	19/06/1916	30/06/1916
Heading	War Diary of Headquarters 40th Divisional Engineers From 1st July 1916 To 31st July 1916 Volume II		
War Diary	Bruay	01/07/1916	04/07/1916
War Diary	Neux Les Mines	05/07/1916	30/10/1916
War Diary	St Michel	31/10/1916	03/11/1916
War Diary	Frohen Le Grand	04/11/1916	04/11/1916
War Diary	Bernaville	05/11/1916	18/11/1916
War Diary	Lesouich	19/11/1916	22/11/1916
War Diary	Doullens	22/11/1916	22/11/1916
War Diary	Canaple	23/11/1916	23/11/1916
War Diary	Ailly Le Haut Clocher	24/11/1916	11/12/1916
War Diary	Maurepas	12/12/1916	14/12/1916
War Diary	Chipilly	15/12/1916	17/12/1916
War Diary	Maurepas	18/12/1916	26/12/1916
War Diary	B16 C Central	27/12/1916	31/12/1916
War Diary	Pc Bonnet	01/01/1917	27/01/1917
War Diary	Corbie	28/01/1917	10/02/1917
War Diary	P C Bonnet	11/02/1917	07/03/1917
War Diary	P C Jean H 1.c. 4.9	08/03/1917	09/03/1917
War Diary	P C Jean	10/03/1917	05/04/1917
War Diary	Manan Court	06/04/1917	05/07/1917
War Diary	Sorel	06/07/1917	17/08/1917
War Diary	Sorel Le Grand	18/08/1917	12/10/1917
War Diary	Haudecourt	13/10/1917	17/10/1917
War Diary	Peronne	18/10/1917	18/10/1917
War Diary	Fosseux	19/10/1917	28/10/1917
War Diary	Peronne	29/10/1917	29/10/1917
War Diary	Equancourt	30/10/1917	31/10/1917
Heading	Vol. 18 War Diary of Headquarters RE		
War Diary	Equancourt	01/11/1917	18/11/1917
War Diary	Haplincourt	19/11/1917	20/11/1917
War Diary	Beaumetz Les-Combrai	21/11/1917	21/11/1917
War Diary	Havrincourt	22/11/1917	02/12/1917
War Diary	Behagnies	03/12/1917	13/12/1917
War Diary	Gomiecourt	14/12/1917	31/12/1917
Miscellaneous	Dear Ponsonby	01/12/1917	01/12/1917
Miscellaneous	40th Div. No. 1073/8. G	04/12/1917	04/12/1917
Miscellaneous	App III Vi Corps Daily Intelligence Summary No. 635	16/12/1917	16/12/1917
Miscellaneous	Headquarters, 119th Infantry Brigade	17/12/1917	17/12/1917

Miscellaneous	40th Division Intelligence Summary No. 27	29/12/1917	29/12/1917
Miscellaneous	40th Division Intelligence Summary No. 29 App VI	31/12/1917	31/12/1917
War Diary	Gomiecourt	01/01/1918	06/01/1918
War Diary	Behagnies	07/01/1918	12/01/1918
War Diary	Gomiecourt	13/02/1918	27/02/1918
War Diary	Basseux	28/02/1918	28/02/1918
Miscellaneous	O.C. 224th. Field Co. RE.	20/01/1918	20/01/1918
Operation(al) Order(s)	40th Division Warning Order No. 127	24/02/1918	24/02/1918
Miscellaneous	O.C. 224th. Field Co. RE.	06/02/1918	06/02/1918
Operation(al) Order(s)	40th Division. Order No. 128	26/02/1918	26/02/1918
Heading	C.R.E. 40th Division March 1918		
War Diary	Basseux	01/03/1918	20/03/1918
War Diary	Hamelincourt	20/03/1918	22/03/1918
War Diary	Gomiecourt	23/03/1918	25/03/1918
War Diary	Bailleulmont And Habarq	26/03/1918	26/03/1918
War Diary	Warluzel	27/03/1918	27/03/1918
War Diary	Lucheux	28/03/1918	28/03/1918
War Diary	Chelers	29/03/1918	31/03/1918
Miscellaneous	VI Corps. No. Gx 599/146	02/03/1918	02/03/1918
Heading	C.R.E. 40th Division April 1918		
Heading	War Diary H Qrs R E 40th Division April 1918		
War Diary	Merville	01/04/1918	01/04/1918
War Diary	Croix De Bac	02/04/1918	08/04/1918
War Diary	Vieux Berquin	09/04/1918	10/04/1918
War Diary	Au Souverain	11/04/1918	12/04/1918
War Diary	Renescure	13/04/1918	13/04/1918
War Diary	Longuenesse	14/04/1918	15/04/1918
War Diary	Wizernes	16/04/1918	22/04/1918
War Diary	Rweld	24/04/1918	30/04/1918
Miscellaneous	Chief Engineers App I	15/04/1918	15/04/1918
Miscellaneous	40th Divisional R.E. Appendix II	09/04/1918	09/04/1918
War Diary	Rweld	01/05/1918	03/06/1918
War Diary	Doornaert	04/06/1918	22/06/1918
War Diary	Renescure	23/06/1918	21/08/1918
War Diary	Near Wallon-Cappel	22/08/1918	31/08/1918
War Diary	Nr Wallon-Cappel	01/09/1918	01/09/1918
War Diary	La Motte	03/09/1918	30/09/1918
War Diary	I Mile W Of Steenwerck	01/10/1918	18/10/1918
War Diary	Armentieres	19/10/1918	19/10/1918
War Diary	Mouvaux	20/10/1918	26/10/1918
War Diary	Lannoy	27/10/1918	31/10/1918
Diagram etc			
Diagram etc	Bridge At L.8.a.5.2 Sheet 36		
Diagram etc	Temporary Bridge Over River At E.26.d.50.37 Sheet 36		
Miscellaneous	To H.Q Ad 40th Division		
War Diary	Lannoy	01/11/1918	23/11/1918
War Diary	Roubaix	25/11/1918	30/11/1918
Diagram etc			
War Diary	Roubaix	01/12/1918	28/02/1919

WO/95/2597/2

Vol 29

WAR DIARY

OF

HEADQUARTERS

40TH DIVISIONAL ENGINEERS

OCTOBER 1918.

VOLUME 29.

1916 JUN — 1919 FEB

RE 40th DW
Vol 1. June

Confidential

War Diary
of
Headquarters
40th Divisional Engineers

from 3rd June 1916 to 30th June 1916.

1

Volume 1.

Feb: 19

Original

Volume 1

Sheet 1

Army Form C. 2118.

Instructions regarding War Diaries and Intelligence Summaries are contained in F. S. Regs., Part II. and the Staff Manual respectively. Title pages will be prepared in manuscript.

WAR DIARY of Headquarters 40th Divisional Engineers
or
~~INTELLIGENCE SUMMARY~~
(Erase heading not required.)

from 3rd June 1916 to 11th June 1916.

Place	Date	Hour	Summary of Events and Information	Remarks and references to Appendices
SOUTHAMPTON	3rd June	7 pm	Embarked on S.S. Huntscraft. Completed 8 pm. alt	
HAVRE	4th	11 am	Disembarked. Completed 3 pm. Proceeded to No 1 Camp. Arrived 4.30 pm. very wet and windy night. Horse lines very much exposed. Exercised horses 2 a.m. alt.	
"	5th	5 pm	Marched to No 3 point GARE DES MARCHANDISES. Arrived 6.15 pm. Entrained. Train left 9 pm. alt.	
ABBEVILLE	6th	7.50 am	Halted for watering etc. (No halt was made at MONTEROLIER BUCHY because train was late) alt.	
LILLERS	"	2 pm	Train arrived. Disentrainment completed 3 pm. alt.	
LIGNY LEZ AIRE	"	5.30 pm	Reached billets at "Mairie." Good cottage billets, with clean beds for officers. School building for office. Good deep well. alt	
"	7th		G.O.C. visited R.E. Billets alt.	
		5.55 pm	Marching Orders received for 231st Coy to proceed to join 1st Div (by Telephone) alt	GAS
"	8th	10 am	231st Coy marched out. alt	
		10.45 am	Movement orders for 229th Co received by telephone, to relieve 70th Field Co at MAZINGARBE, to move by 'bus, Officers in Motor car. alt	
		11.50 am	Telephone message received from G.S. "One officer 229 Co to proceed today to take over". alt	
		6.55 pm	224 Coys move to 15th Div Telephone Message. All arrangements to be made by C.R.Es. C.R.E. and Adjt to visit 15th Div for 4 days and 1st & 16th Div for visit. alt	
"	9th	7.45 pm	229 Coy busses started. alt One officer 224 Co went to 15th Div to arrange billets etc. returning in evening. alt	
		3.40 pm	Orders by telephone. 224 Co to move to 15th Div on <u>12th</u> June. alt C.E. 1st Corps visited C.R.E. alt	
"	10th	9.5 am	Party for instruction in Hydraulic Pipe Pusher left. Bus sent could only carry 25. 33 in party, so 8 went on cycles, Hence delay ½ hour alt	
		3.30 pm	Visited by G.S.O. 1. alt	
"	11th		Details of 229th & 231st Field Coys proceeded to join their companies. alt	

R J B Mair
Lt Col RE
CRE 40th Div

2353 Wt. W2544/1454 700,000 5/15 D. D. & L. A.D.S.S./Forms/C. 2118.

Original.

Sheet 2

Army Form C. 2118.

Instructions regarding War Diaries and Intelligence Summaries are contained in F. S. Regs., Part II. and the Staff Manual respectively. Title pages will be prepared in manuscript.

WAR DIARY for Headquarters 40th Divisional Engineers from June 12th 1916.

~~INTELLIGENCE SUMMARY.~~

(Erase heading not required.)

Place	Date	Hour	Summary of Events and Information	Remarks and references to Appendices
LIGNY LEZ AIRE	June 12th	9 am	One Officer 224th Co left in motorcar to join 15th Div. ALt	
		12 noon	224 Co started in 7 busses ~~to~~ join 15th Div. ALt	
"	13th		Nil. ALt	
"	14th	11 am	C.R.E. started by motorcar to join 15th Div. ALt	
"	15th		Nil ALt	
"	16th	5.15 pm	Div Order No 1 received to "concentrate". ALt	
"	17th	8. am	Q orders received Field Coys get in touch with Staff Capts of Bdes. ALt	
"		2.45 pm	C.R.E. returned. ALt	
"	18th	7 am	Adjt & Interpreter left for BRUAY to arrange billets, returning 5 pm. ALt	
"	19th	8.10 am	Marched out ALt	
BRUAY	"	12 noon	Arrived and took over billets at once. Office 9 Rue Nationale. Officers Nos 5A, 7A, 15, 18, men and horses in Stables of Hotel Moderne. ALt	
"	20th	—	Adjt visited C.R.E. 1st Div. ALt	
"	21st	—	Routine work ALt	
"	22nd	—	C.R.E. proceeded to BETHUNE & NOEUX to visit Army workshops and C.R.E. 1st Div. ALt	
"	23rd	—	Adjt visited C.R.E. 16th Div and examined Pt SAINS – BARLIN Road. also examined crater K18C 5.8. ("B" already made) ALt [Map – FRANCE Sheet 36B scale 1/40000]	
"	24th	—	Routine work. ALt	
"	25th	—	Routine work. ALt	
"	26th	—	Routine work ALt	
"	27th	—	C.R.E. visited C.R.E. 16th Div and 231st Fd Co at Les BREBIS. ALt	
"	28th	—	Adjt visited R.E. Park at LILLERS.	
"		7.30 pm	224 Coy reported arrival in 121st Bde area. ALt	

R. P. Main
Lieut Col. R.E.
C.R.E. 40th Div

Original

Sheet 3

Army Form C. 2118.

Instructions regarding War Diaries and Intelligence Summaries are contained in F. S. Regs., Part II. and the Staff Manual respectively. Title pages will be prepared in manuscript.

WAR DIARY
or
~~INTELLIGENCE SUMMARY.~~

of Headquarters 40th Divisional Engineers from 29th June 1916 to 30th June 1916.

(Erase heading not required.)

Place	Date	Hour	Summary of Events and Information	Remarks and references to Appendices
BRUAY	29.6.16		C.R.E. visited 1st Corps Yard MINX. A.W.	
"	30.6.16		Routine work.	
			229th Field Coy rejoined Division and took billets in BRUAY. Sheet 36B — J.10.c	
			231st Field Coy rejoined the Division and took billets in LA CAUCHIETTE. A.W. Sheet 36B I.23.d	

HEADQUARTERS * 1 - JUL. 1916 * 40th DIVISION R.E.

R J W Mair
Lieut Col RE.
30.6.16 CRE 40th Div.

40 July

CRE. 40 D.V.

Vol 2

War Diary

of

Head Quarters

40th Divisional Engineers

from 1st July 1916 to 31st July 1916.

Volume II

Army Form C. 2118.

Instructions regarding War Diaries and Intelligence Summaries are contained in F. S. Regs., Part II. and the Staff Manual respectively. Title pages will be prepared in manuscript.

WAR DIARY or ~~INTELLIGENCE SUMMARY.~~ of Headquarters 40th Div Engineers from 1st July 1916 till 9.7.16

(Erase heading not required.)

Place	Date	Hour	Summary of Events and Information	Remarks and references to Appendices
BRUAY	1.7.16		Routine work. Alt	
	2.7.16	11 am	Intimation received of movement to relieve 1st Div. Alt	
		2 pm	C.R.E. proceeded in motor car to arrange moves etc with C.R.E. 1st Div. Alt	
		7 pm	40th Div Order No 2 received:— detailed orders for the relief of 1st Div in Right Sector 1st Corps. Alt	
"	3.7.16	10 am	C.R.E. & Adjt went in motor to take over from 1st D.E. at NEUX les MINES and LES BREBIS, returning to BRUAY, CRE at 5 pm, Adjt at 7 pm. C.R.E. 1st Div visited billets etc at BRUAY at 7 pm, & returned. Alt	
"	4.7.16	7 am	Advanced party started for NEUX les MINES. arrived 9 am. Alt	
		10 am	C.R.E. started in motor. Remainder of Hdqrs D.E. by road. arrived NEUX at 12.30 pm. CRE 1st Div & adjt went away in motor at about 2.30 pm. 1st DE Hqrs marched out about 1 pm.	Alt
NEUX LES MINES	5.7.16	10 am	C.R.E. & adjt went in motor to LES BREBIS. Visited all Field Coys and D.E. store. Returned 1.15 pm. Alt	
		4.30 pm	Adjt went to MINX to ascertain supplies of stores available. Returned 7.30 pm. Alt	
"	6.7.16		Routine work. Looked through stores in D.E. Yard. Visited Field Coys, arranged requisitions for issue of stores.	
		11.30 am	Adjt went (on horse) to LES BREBIS. Returned 4.45 pm. Alt. 4. pm Chaplain went to 224th Co to spend a few days. Alt	
"	7.7.16	10. am	C.E. 1st Corps visited the office and discussed trench work, stores etc. Alt	
		11. am	C.R.E. started in car to visit 197 Co at BETHUNE and O/c R.E. Stores, MINX. Alt	
		4 pm	The mine buildings were slightly shelled about 6 shells, (3 blind). Alt	
"	8.7.16	10 am	Capt Collins arrived to discuss his section of the line, MAROC, with C.R.E. Returned 3 pm. Alt	
"	9.7.16	10 am	C.R.E. started to go round trenches with G.S.O.I. Examined Right Sector CALONNE. Returned 4 pm. Alt	
		11am	Adjt went to Stores LES BREBIS, returned 2.30 pm.	
		3pm	& went to MINX to arrange supply of stores, and to deposit with MINX duplicate of a signed indent lost by R.A. Returned 5.30 pm. Alt	

Army Form C. 2118.

Instructions regarding War Diaries and Intelligence Summaries are contained in F. S. Regs., Part II. and the Staff Manual respectively. Title pages will be prepared in manuscript.

WAR DIARY of Headquarters or ~~INTELLIGENCE SUMMARY.~~ 40th Divisional Engineers from 10th July 1916 to 16th July 1916

(Erase heading not required.)

Place	Date	Hour	Summary of Events and Information	Remarks and references to Appendices
NEUX LES MINES	10th		Routine work	
		2 pm	Adjt went in car to MINX returning 2.40 pm. (i) to find out why R.A. could get no material (ii) to arrange for extra supplies of R.E. stores, and order 50 "parrying sticks" and two traversing frames for telescopes in O.P.s required by G.S.O.3. ACH	
	11th	10 am	B. Gen R.A. came in to discuss indenting and supply of R.E. stores for gunpits etc. ACH	
		2 pm	Adjt went to LES BREBIS (horse) inspected stores in D.E. yard. Went to each coy in turn and explained shortage of timber, need for ordering special stores early etc. A good supply of stores came in by train. Salvage of R.E. Stores becoming very effective — especially damaged but repairable tools etc brought in by parties returning from trenches etc. Returned 6.30 pm. ACH	
	12th	2 pm	C.R.E. went to LES BREBIS in car, returned 5.30 pm. ACH	
	13th	9.30 am	C.R.E. went to LES BREBIS in car with G.S.O. to go round trenches. Returned 4 pm. ACH Went round "reserve line" & "village line" etc. ACH	
		2 pm	Adjt went on horse to LES BREBIS to store yard. Visited 229th Field Co. Selected Rails etc for issue to R.A. Reserve enclosure in D E yard commenced. Returned 5.45 pm. ACH	
		2.30 pm	Medical Officer went to LES BREBIS to join 231st Field Co, taking with him maltese cart, two medical orderlies, and batman. ACH	
	14th	2 pm	C.R.E. went in car to MINX and BETHUNE WORKSHOPS. ACH	
		3 pm	Adjt went to D.E. yard & 229th Field Co returned 6.45 pm. No train had come in to the yard. ACH	
	15th	11 am	Adjt went on horse to HOUCHIN to see Infantry horse shelters. Returned 1 pm. ACH	
	16th	11 am	Adjt went in ambulance to Divisional Laundry — inspected & tuned petrol engine. Visited Army Workshops BETHUNE, drew some iron trench frames for BURNING BING, and some tin notice boards. Visited MINX to see telescope traversing frames which had been wrongly made. Returned 2-30 pm. ACH	
		3.30 pm	Adjt went on horse to LES BREBIS to D.E. Yard. Good train load in. Great difficulty in meeting Gunners demands for heavy stores — rails, timber etc. Arranged party to repair horse standings at HOUCHIN for Infantry transport. Returned 7.30 pm. ACH	

Instructions regarding War Diaries and Intelligence Summaries are contained in F. S. Regs., Part II. and the Staff Manual respectively. Title pages will be prepared in manuscript.

Army Form C. 2118.

WAR DIARY or ~~INTELLIGENCE SUMMARY.~~ of Headquarters 40th Divisional Engineers from 17th July 1916 to 24th July 1916

(Erase heading not required.)

Place	Date	Hour	Summary of Events and Information	Remarks and references to Appendices
NEUX les MINES	17th	9.30am	Adjt went on horse to HOUCHIN to see progress on Infantry Transport Shelters, afterwards to D.A.C. at HESDIGNEUL to inspect roofs of shelters which required re-tarring, to HALLICOURT to D.S.C. workshop, HOUCHIN, MINX. Returned 5 pm. ACT	
		10 am.	C.R.E. went in car to LES BREBIS. Went round CALONNE DEFENCES with O.C. 12th YORKS Pioneer Batn. Visited all 3 Field Coys. Returned 7 pm. ACT	
	18th	~~2.30pm~~ 11 am	G.O.C. came in to C.R.E's office and discussed defences etc for about 1 hour. ACT	
		2.30pm	Adjt went on horse to LES BREBIS. Visited Mine Offices to try to buy rails – without success. Visited Storeyard, 231st Fd Co, 229th Fd Co, met O.C. 224th Fd Co. Returned 7 pm. ACT One horse shod at 231st Coy. ACT	
	19th	2 pm	C.R.E. went in car to BETHUNE, Army Workshop. and MINX, with OC. 224th Field Coy. ACT	
		3 pm	Adjt went on horse to LES BREBIS, D.E. yard, and 231st Field Co. ACT	
	20th	2 pm	C.R.E. went in car to go round trenches with O.C. 12th Yorks Pioneer Batn. ACT	
		3 pm	Adjt went to LES BREBIS R.E. yard. Trouble with unloading parties – morning party taken by 197th Coy for work on water supply. 2nd Party asked for from 119th Bde had no instructions (i) to whom to report, (ii) for what purpose. Visited 231st Co and 229th. One horse shod at 229th Co. ACT	
	21st		Orders received to make arrangements for taking over LOOS sector.	
		2.30pm	C.R.E. 16th Div came to discuss the taking over, & to arrange relief of R.E. at LOOS. ACT	
		3.45pm	CRE 40th Div went in car to LES BREBIS to 224th Fd Coy. ACT	
	22nd		No working party obtainable to unload stores in DE Yard.	
		5pm	Adjt went to D.E Yard. Tried to get working party. Finally arranged with 8th Ry Co that trucks would be left and unloaded next morning. ACT	
	23rd	2 pm	C.R.E. went in car to LES BREBIS. Visited companies. ACT	
		3 pm	Adjt went to LES BREBIS to D.E. Yard. All stores unloaded. One horse shod at 229th Coy. ACT	
	24th		Routine work. Adjt visited Divl Laundry to inspect belting of machinery, said to require renewal. ACT	

Army Form C. 2118.

Instructions regarding War Diaries and Intelligence Summaries are contained in F. S. Regs., Part II. and the Staff Manual respectively. Title pages will be prepared in manuscript.

WAR DIARY or ~~INTELLIGENCE SUMMARY~~ of Headquarters 40th Divisional Engineers from 25th July 1916 to 31st July 1916.

(Erase heading not required.)

Place	Date	Hour	Summary of Events and Information	Remarks and references to Appendices
NEUX LES MINES	25	9 am	Adjt went in Lorry to MINX to arrange supply of stores. Proceeded to 1st Army workshop BETHUNE. Drew a lorry full of stores including 2 Batteries, Rifle grenade, for 8 rifles & 10 single stands, sniperscopes, speaking tubes etc. ACT.	
	26th	9 am	Adjt went in lorry to BETHUNE army workshop and drew 3 Batteries, rifle grenade, and 20 single stands. ACT	
		2 pm	C.R.E. visited all companies at LES BREBIS. ACT.	
	27th	9 30	C.R.E. went to meet C.E. 1st Corps to go round trenches. ACT	
		3 pm	Adjt went to MAROC to convey G.O.C.s instructions to O.C. Pioneer Batn [Yorks] clearing communication trenches. ACT.	
	28th	2-30 pm	C.R.E. & adjt went to LES BREBIS. Returned 4-30 pm. Adjt continued to RUITZ to find ½ Coy from 32nd Div and give instructions for joining 40th Divl Engineers at LES BREBIS. Returned 5-45 pm. ACT.	
	29th	9 am	C.R.E. went round trenches with G.O.C. returned 3 pm. ACT.	
		3 pm	Adjt went to MINX, arranged supply of watering troughs & dugout casings. ACT. 2 sections from 32nd Div attached to 229th Field Co for work in reserve line etc. ACT.	
	30th	2.30 pm	Adjt went to HOUCHIN to inspect huts, and to MINX. ACT	
	31st	2-15 pm	C.R.E. went in car to LES BREBIS. visited Pioneers working on dugouts, and 229th & 231st Field Coys. ACT.	
		3 pm	Adjt went to MINX and 1st Army Workshop BETHUNE. ACT.	

R. J. B[illegible]
Lieut Col. RE
CRE 40th Divn.

2353 Wt. W2544/1454 700,000 5/15 D. D. & L. A.D.S.S./Forms/C. 2118.

Sheet 1

Instructions regarding War Diaries and Intelligence Summaries are contained in F. S. Regs., Part II. and the Staff Manual respectively. Title pages will be prepared in manuscript.

WAR DIARY or ~~INTELLIGENCE SUMMARY.~~ of Headquarters 40th Divisional Engineers from 1st August 1916

(*Erase heading not required.*)

Army Form C. 2118.

Place	Date	Hour	Summary of Events and Information	Remarks and references to Appendices
NEUX LES MINES	1st	12 noon	Adjt went to LES BREBIS, D.E. Yard, visited 231st & 229th Field Coys. Examined watering arrangements of RFA waggon lines near Fosse 2 & BETHUNE, where more troughs are required.	A.W.H.
			C.R.E. went to the battle area of the SOMME with C.R.A. and G.S.O.1.	A.W.H.
	2nd	7.30 am		
	3rd	2.30 pm	C.R.E. went to BETHUNE to meet 2nd Lt BORRIE R.E. who arrived as a reinforcement for 229th Field Coy. C.R.E. then proceeded to LES BREBIS.	A.W.H.
		3. pm	Adjt proceeded to visit Corps Brickstack R10b08, D.E. Yard, Field Companies, and Hants AT Co.	A.W.H.
	4th		Routine work	A.W.H.
	5th	2.15 pm	CRE went to MAROC	A.W.H.
	6th		Routine Work	A.W.H.
	7th		Routine Work	A.W.H.
	8th	[illegible]	CRE proceeded to BETHUNE and MINX	A.W.H.
	9th	2.30 pm	CRE proceeded to MINX, BETHUNE, LES BREBIS, and MAROC.	A.W.H.
	10th	10.30 am	Adjt proceeded to LES BREBIS to hand over stores in R.E. Yard to Lieut Denton RE. CRE proceeded to [illegible] Bouvière [illegible]	A.W.H.
	11th	10.30 pm	Lieut Denton reported at 10.0 am to take over duties of adjutant. CRE proceeded to Minx [illegible]	[illegible]
	12th	10.30	Capt [illegible] left at 11 [illegible] to join the 2[illegible] Field Coy RE at [illegible] CRE proceeded [illegible] [illegible] proceeded to Les Brebis [illegible] [illegible] of [illegible]	[illegible]

2353 Wt. W2544/1454 700,000 5/15 D. D. & L. A.D.S.S./Forms/C. 2118.

Sheet 2

Instructions regarding War Diaries and Intelligence Summaries are contained in F. S. Regs., Part II. and the Staff Manual respectively. Title pages will be prepared in manuscript.

WAR DIARY
or
INTELLIGENCE SUMMARY.
(Erase heading not required.)

Army Form C. 2118.

Headquarters
40th Divisional RE
August 1916

Place	Date	Hour	Summary of Events and Information	Remarks and references to Appendices
NEOUX les Mines	13th	9-30pm	CRE proceeded to Les Brebis. Adjutant proceeded to DEYAUD les Brebis and also to Minx	JD
	14th	10-30	CRE attended Divisional conference. Adjt proceeded to Les Brebis and Minx	JD
–	15th	10-30	Morning spent in routine work. CRE and Adjt proceeded to Les Brebis Minx Divisional Baths and to the distillery on the NEOUX–BARLIN Road. It was reported at 8pm that 2Lt Peacock 224th had been killed by shell fire	JD
–	16th	10.0	Morning spent in routine work. Adjutant proceeded to Les Brebis and Minx	JD
–	17th	10.0	Morning spent in routine work. Adjutant proceeded to Minx and Bethune in the afternoon	JD
–	18th	10-15	Morning routine work. Adjt proceeded to Maroc & CRE attended Div'l conference afternoon	JD
–	19th	10-45	Routine work. CRE proceeded to Les Brebis in the evening	JD
–	20th	10-30	Adjt proceeded to Les Brebis morning. CRE proceeded to MAROC afternoon routine work	JD
–	21st	10-30	routine work	JD
–	22nd	10-30	CRE proceeded to Maroc routine work – Mine	JD
–	23	10-30	OC 231st Coy came to Neoux to consult CRE. CRE & Adjt proceeded to Les Brebis to 229th Coy & thence to Petit Sains to visit CRE 15th Div	JD
–	24	10-15	Routine work, CRE proceeded to the RE 16th Div to [illegible]	JD

2353 Wt. W2544/1454 700,000 5/15 D. D. & L. A.D.S.S./Forms/C. 2118.

Headquarters 40th Divisional R.E. August 1916 — Army Form C. 2118. — Sheet 3

Instructions regarding War Diaries and Intelligence Summaries are contained in F. S. Regs., Part II. and the Staff Manual respectively. Title pages will be prepared in manuscript.

WAR DIARY
or
INTELLIGENCE SUMMARY.
(Erase heading not required.)

Place	Date	Hour	Summary of Events and Information	Remarks and references to Appendices
NEOUX LES MINES	25/8/16	10-0	CRE and adjutant proceeded to Lillers to arrange affairs of [illegible] [illegible] [illegible] for RE Stores also to visit Army RE [illegible] [illegible] [illegible] conference at H.Q. [illegible] at 5.30	[initials]
—	26/8/16	10-30	Routine work Adjutant proceeded to [illegible] CRE proceeded to [illegible]	[initials]
—	27/8/16	10-30	CRE [illegible] [illegible] [illegible] Adjt. proceeded to [illegible] [illegible] the RE Stores there	[initials]
—	28/8/16	10-0	Routine work CRE proceeded to [illegible]	[initials]
—	29/8/16	10-30	Routine work Adjt proceeded to [illegible] [illegible]	[initials]
—	30/8/16	10-30	Routine work CRE proceeded to [illegible]	[initials]
—	31/8/16	10-0	Routine work	[initials]

R. [illegible]
Lieut Col. RE
CRE 40th Division
31.8.16

2353 Wt. W2544/1454 700,000 5/15 D. D. & L. A.D.S.S./Forms/C. 2118.

Instructions regarding War Diaries and Intelligence Summaries are contained in F. S. Regs., Part II. and the Staff Manual respectively. Title pages will be prepared in manuscript.

Army Form C. 2118.

WAR DIARY
or
~~INTELLIGENCE SUMMARY.~~
(Erase heading not required.)

September 1916 HQ 40th Divisional Engineers

Place	Date	Hour	Summary of Events and Information	Remarks and references to Appendices
Noeux les Mines	1/9/16	10-0	Routine work Adjt proceeded to Les Brebis	JD
—	2/9/16	10-0		
—	3/9/16	10-0	Routine work. One man out of 8 advised arrived for instruction in pipe pushing. Adjt proceeded to Les Brebis & Grenay	JD
—	4/9/16	10-0	Routine work in office afternoon Adjt proceeded to mines Party of men reported for instructing Field Coys in Pipe Pushing	JD
—	5/9/16	10-0	Routine work CRE proceeded to Les Brebis & Grenay	JD
—	6/9/16	10-45	Adjt proceeded to Hallicourt & mine	JD
—	7/9/16	10-30	CRE & Adjt proceeded to Bethune & Auchel	JD
—	8/9/16	10-0	CRE proceeded to Les Brebis & Grenay Adjt proceeded to mines	JD
—	9/9/16	10-0	CRE and Adjutant proceeded to Houchin to investigate methods of boring in chalk Capt Rait Kerr reported to take command of 231st Fd Coy RE	JD
—	10/9/16	10-30	CRE proceeded to Bethune Major Pears visited CRE & went to 224th Coy	JD
—	11/9/16	10-0	CRE proceeded to Les Brebis	JD
—	12/9/16	9-30	CRE proceeded to Loos with GOC Capt Rait Kerr's appointment to 231st cancelled Major Pears left Division for 30th Div	JD
—	13/9/16	11-0	CRE and Adjt proceeded to investigate boring apparatus	JD

Army Form C. 2118.

WAR DIARY

or

~~INTELLIGENCE SUMMARY.~~

(Erase heading not required.)

Instructions regarding War Diaries and Intelligence Summaries are contained in F. S. Regs., Part II. and the Staff Manual respectively. Title pages will be prepared in manuscript.

September 1916 Contd. — HQ 40th Divisional Engineers

Place	Date	Hour	Summary of Events and Information	Remarks and references to Appendices
Necoux les Mines	27/9/16	9-30	Adjt proceeded to Mieux & Bethune CRE proceeded to Les Brebis & Maroc	J.D.
—	28/9/16	10-0	Routine work	J.D.
—	29/9/16	10-0	Adjt proceeded to Mieux CE 1st visited CRE	J.D.
—	30/9/16	10-0	Capt Miller reported & took over command of 224th (Fd) Coy RE. CRE proceeded to Houdain to inspect work on boring, Bethune & Mieux	J.D.

[signature] Lieut RE
Adjt 40th DE

2353 Wt. W2544/1454 700,000 5/15 D. D. & L. A.D.S.S./Forms/C. 2118.

Instructions regarding War Diaries and Intelligence Summaries are contained in F. S. Regs., Part II. and the Staff Manual respectively. Title pages will be prepared in manuscript.

WAR DIARY
or
INTELLIGENCE SUMMARY.
(Erase heading not required.)

Army Form C. 2118.

HQ 40th Divisional Engrs — Oct 1916

Place	Date	Hour	Summary of Events and Information	Remarks and references to Appendices
Noeux les Mines	1/10/16	10-0	Adjt proceeded to MINX CRE to Les Brebis	J.D.
—	2/10/16	9-30	Routine work.	J.D.
—	3/10/16	10-0	Routine work CRE proceeded to Les Brebis	J.D.
—	4/10/16	10-15	CE 1st Corps visited billets etc of Field Coys with CRE Adjt proceeded to Mazingarbe Les Brebis MINX	J.D.
—	5/10/16	9-30	Adjt proceeded to Labussiere Bethune & Minx	J.D.
—	6/10/16	9-45	CRE proceeded to Les Brebis & Maroc Adjt to Minx	J.D.
—	7/10/16	10-0	CRE proceeded to Les Brebis & Maroc.	J.D.
—	8/10/16	10-0	RSM Cook goes sick & CSM Court takes over DE yard temporarily CRE to Les Brebis to make arrangements for handing over S Maroc & taking over Hulluch to Boyau 77	J.D.
—	9/10/16	9-30	Routine work	J.D.
—	10/10/16	9-15	CRE & Adjt proceeded to Sailly Labourse to take over from 8th Div the Section Posen alley to Boyau 77, to Philosophe to view Fosse 3 dump & billets & HQ of 231st Fd Coy RE then to Sains Gohelle to hand over S Maroc to 37th Div	J.D.
	11/10/16	9-45	The whole Division side steps. 224th leave S MAROC & take over part of LOOS	J.D.
	12/10/16	10-0	229th take over 14 BIS & 231st take over line to BOYAU 77 from 8th Division	

2353 Wt. W2544/1454 700,000 5/15 D. D. & L. A.D.S.S./Forms/C. 2118.

Instructions regarding War Diaries and Intelligence Summaries are contained in F. S. Regs., Part II. and the Staff Manual respectively. Title pages will be prepared in manuscript.

WAR DIARY
or
INTELLIGENCE SUMMARY.
(Erase heading not required.)

Army Form C. 2118.

Place	Date	Hour	Summary of Events and Information	Remarks and references to Appendices
Noeux les Mines	13/10/16	10-0	Morning routine work Afternoon CRE proceeded to MINX and BETHUNE —	J.D.
—	14/10/16	10-0	CRE proceeded to MAROC adjt to MINX —	J.D.
—	15/10/16	10-0	Routine work —	J.D.
—	16/10/16	10-0	CRE attended conference at Corps HQ —	J.D.
—	17/10/16	10-0	CRE proceeded to LES BREBIS and PHILOSOPHE —	J.D.
—	18/10/16	9-30.	Routine work CRE proceeded to BETHUNE, CAPT Johnson [illegible] Coy came in from PHILOSOPHE to consult CRE on work in hand ADJT paraded HQ staff	J.D.
—	19/10/16	9-30	Routine work CRE 24th Division visited CRE to discuss the sector —	J.D.
—	20/10/16	10-0	Routine work CRE proceeded to PHILOSOPHE + adjt to LES BREBIS —	J.D.
—	21/10/16	10-0	Adjt proceeded to MINX CRE to MAZINGARBE arrangements made for the detached men to rejoin their units —	J.D.
—	22/10/16	9-30	Adjt 24th Div came to look over the stores at DEyard CRE proceeded to PHILOSOPHE —	J.D.
—	23/10/16	9-30	Routine work —	J.D.
—	24/10/16	9-30	Routine work arranging move of Field Coys —	J.D.
—	25/10/16	9-30		

Instructions regarding War Diaries and Intelligence Summaries are contained in F. S. Regs., Part II. and the Staff Manual respectively. Title pages will be prepared in manuscript.

WAR DIARY
or
INTELLIGENCE SUMMARY.
(Erase heading not required.)

Army Form C. 2118.

Place	Date	Hour	Summary of Events and Information	Remarks and references to Appendices
NOEUX LES MINES	26th/10/16	10.0	Routine work arrangements for handing over to 24th DE completed –	[illegible]
	27/10/16	10.0		
—	28/10/16	10-0	Routine work	[illegible]
—	29/10/16	10-0		
—	30/10/16	10-0	Today CRE handed over the section [illegible] 14 Bis [illegible] to CRE 24th Div. 8.30 am HQ marched off to St MICHEL to prepare for the march of Div to Reserve Army	[illegible]
St MICHEL	31/10/16	9.0	St MICHEL	[illegible]

R. [illegible]
Lieut Col. RE
CRE 40th Div

2353 Wt. W2544/1454 700,000 5/15 D. D. & L. A.D.S.S./Forms/C. 2118.

Army Form C. 2118.

WAR DIARY
or
INTELLIGENCE SUMMARY.
(*Erase heading not required.*)

Instructions regarding War Diaries and Intelligence Summaries are contained in F. S. Regs., Part II. and the Staff Manual respectively. Title pages will be prepared in manuscript.

HQ 40th Divisional Engrs   November 1916

Place	Date	Hour	Summary of Events and Information	Remarks and references to Appendices
St MICHEL	1/11/16	10.0	Have settled in here & received orders we are not to move till 4th	J.D.
–	2/11/16 3/11/16	10-0	ST MICHEL	J.D.
FROHEN LE GRAND	4/11/16	10.0	HQRE marched from St MICHEL at 9.0 via St POL + LIGNY SUR CAUCHE to FROHEN LE GRAND	J.D.
BERNAVILLE	5/11/16	10.0	Marched from FROHEN LE GRAND to BERNAVILLE	J.D.
–	6/11/16 7/11/16	10.0	BERNAVILLE	J.D.
–	8/11/16			
–	9/11/16			
–	10/11/16		"	
–	11/11/16			
–	12/11/16			
–	13/11/16			
–	14/11/16		"	
–	15/11/16		We march with Divisional HQ to FROHEN LE GRAND via HERZECOURT	J.D.
	16/11/16 17/11/16 18/11/16		FROHEN LE GRAND	J.D.

2353 Wt. W2544/1454 700,000 5/15 D. D. & L. A.D.S.S./Forms/C. 2118.

Army Form C. 2118.

Instructions regarding War Diaries and Intelligence Summaries are contained in F. S. Regs., Part II. and the Staff Manual respectively. Title pages will be prepared in manuscript.

WAR DIARY
or
INTELLIGENCE SUMMARY.

(Erase heading not required.)

Place	Date	Hour	Summary of Events and Information	Remarks and references to Appendices
LESOUICH	19.11.16	10/0	We proceed from FROHEN LE GRAND by way of BARLY and BOUQUEMAISON leaving at 11 AM and arriving at LE SOUICH at 1-30 pm	FD
"	20/11/16	8.0	LE SOUICH	FD
"	21/11/16	8.0		
DOULLENS	22/11/16	9.0	We proceed to DOULLENS by way of BOUQUEMAISON and arrived there 12-15 pm CRE proceeded on leave at 6 pm by way of AMIENS. Capt ORMISTON of the 229th Fd Coy RE takes duties of acting CRE but not to leave his Coy.	FD
CANAPLE	23/11/16	10.0	We proceed to CANAPLE by way of CANDAS arriving at 4 pm	FD
AILLY LE HAUT CLOCHER	24/11/16	10.0	We proceed to AILLY LE HAUT CLOCHER by way of DOMART EN PONTHIERE arriving 4 pm	FD
"	25/11/16	10.0	AILLY LE HAUT CLOCHER	FD
"	26/11/16	10.0	Acting CRE visits CE XV CORPS and makes arrangements for material for Improvement of billets in this area. Lieut E WILBORN joins HQ RE to assist Adjutant	FD
"	27, 28, 29, 30/11/16		AILLY LE HAUT CLOCHER	FD

Frank Denton Lt RE
Adj 40th DE
30/11/16

2353 Wt. W2544/1454 700,000 5/15 D. D. & L. A.D.S.S./Forms/C. 2118.

(1)

Army Form C. 2118.

WAR DIARY
or
~~INTELLIGENCE SUMMARY.~~
(Erase heading not required.)

Instructions regarding War Diaries and Intelligence Summaries are contained in F. S. Regs., Part II. and the Staff Manual respectively. Title pages will be prepared in manuscript.

HdQ. 40th Divl Engineers — December 1916

Place	Date	Hour	Summary of Events and Information	Remarks and references to Appendices
AILLY. LE HAUT CLOCHER	1/12/16 2/12/16 3/12/16		} AILLY LE HAUT CLOCHER	EW
	4/12/16	10pm	CRE returned from leave	EW
	5/12/16			
	6/12/16	7.30 pm	Lieut. & Denton ^Adjutant proceeded on leave from Dec 7.	EW
	7/12/16			
	8/12/16			
	9/12/16	10 AM	Proceeded from Ailly le Haut Clocher to ST SAVOUR arriving 4pm	EW
	10/12/16	8 AM	" " St Savour to SAILLY LE SEC by way of CORBIE arriving 8-30pm CRE proceeded to CHIPILLY	EW
	11/12/16	9 AM	Proceeded from Sailly le Sec to MAUREPAS by way of BRAY MARICOURT & HARDICOURT arrived 4-30 PM CRE arrived earlier & returned to CHIPILLY.	EW
MAUREPAS	12/12/16			
	13/12/16	8 AM	Proceeded from MAUREPAS to CHIPILLY via BRAY & ETINGHAM arriving 2-30pm	EW
	14/12/16	11 AM	CRE proceeded to MAUREPAS	EW
CHIPILLY	15/12/16			
	16/12/16			
	17/12/16	8 AM	Proceeded to MAUREPAS arriving 1 PM	EW
MAUREPAS	18/12/16			
	19/12/16		CRE met CE XVth Corps & inspected scheme of defence. Adjutant returned from leave	EW.
	20/12/16		} Routine Work	JD
"	2?/12/16			
"	26/12/16		Adjt proceeded to 33rd Division RE HQ to arrange for taking over Stores —	JD

2353 Wt. W2544/1454 700,000 5/15 D. D. & L. A.D.S.S./Forms/C. 2118.

(2)

Instructions regarding War Diaries and Intelligence Summaries are contained in F. S. Regs., Part II. and the Staff Manual respectively. Title pages will be prepared in manuscript.

WAR DIARY
or
~~INTELLIGENCE SUMMARY.~~
(Erase heading not required.)

Army Form C. 2118.

Dec. 1916

Place	Date	Hour	Summary of Events and Information	Remarks and references to Appendices
B16 C Central	27/12/16	10-0	Lt E Wilburn proceeded to take over from CRE 33rd Division [illegible] arranged for by CRE 40th Division. CRE takes over the 33rd Division Area and his office is established at B16C central	[initials]
"	28/12/16	10-0	Routine work	[initials]
"	29/12/16			
"	30/12/16	10-0	CRE 8th Division visited CRE. Lt E Wilburn rejoins 231st Fd Coy RE	[initials]
"	31/12/16	9-0	Routine work.	[initials]

R. J. [illegible]
Lieut Col RE
CRE 40th Divn.

2353 Wt. W2544/1454 700,000 5/15 D. D. & L. A.D.S.S./Forms/C. 2118.

Instructions regarding War Diaries and Intelligence Summaries are contained in F. S. Regs., Part II. and the Staff Manual respectively. Title pages will be prepared in manuscript.

Army Form C. 2118.

WAR DIARY
or
~~INTELLIGENCE SUMMARY~~.
(*Erase heading not required.*)

Hd Quarters 40th Divisional Engineers Jan 1917

Place	Date	Hour	Summary of Events and Information	Remarks and references to Appendices
PC BONNET	1/1/17	9/0	Routine work	[illegible]
	2/1/17	17/0	CRE attends Corps conference held at Divisional Headquarters	[illegible]
"	3/1/17	10/0	Routine work	[illegible]
"	4/1/17	10/0	Lieut Cairns 12th Bn Yorks Regt. reported for attachment to CRE	[illegible]
	5/1/17		Routine work.	[illegible]
	6/1/17			
	7/1/17		Routine work	[illegible]
	8/1/17	10-0		
	9/1/17			
	10/1/17		Routine work.	[illegible]
	11/1/17			[illegible]
	12/1/17		CRE attends Corps conference	
	13/1/17		CRE walks over intermediate line & trench area South	[illegible]
	14/1/17		Routine work in office	
	15/1/17		CRE proceeded to Etinehem to take over the duties of CE XV Corps. Lt Col Becher takes over the position of CRE 40th Division during absence of Lt Col Mair RE	[illegible]
	16/1/17		Routine work	[illegible]
	17/1/17			

Instructions regarding War Diaries and Intelligence Summaries are contained in F. S. Regs., Part II. and the Staff Manual respectively. Title pages will be prepared in manuscript.

WAR DIARY
or
INTELLIGENCE SUMMARY.

Army Form C. 2118.

(Erase heading not required.)

Headquarters 40th Divisional Engineers

Place	Date	Hour	Summary of Events and Information	Remarks and references to Appendices
~~Bonnet~~ BONNET	18/1/17 19/1/17 20/1/17 21/1/17		Routine work	[initials]
–	22/1/17 23/1/17		Routine work.	
–	24/1/17		CRE 8th Division came to these HQ to discuss the taking over	[initials]
–	25/1/17 26/1/17		Routine work.	[initials]
–	27/1/17		Preparing reports for handing over to CRE 8th Division	[initials]
CORBIE	28/1/17		HQ move back to middle area transport leaves at 9.30 & Adjt leaves at 11/30 when CRE 8th Division takes over work office opened at CORBIE	[initials]
–	29/1/17		CRE is taken sick with a chill. Adjt takes steps to form small dumps for improvements of CORBIE area & arranges to take over small dump belonging to the 238 (AT) Coy RE	[initials]
	30/1/17 31/1/17		Routine work CRE sick	[initials]

[signature] Lt RE
Adjt 40th DE

2353 Wt. W2544/1454 700,000 5/15 D. D. & L. A.D.S.S./Forms/C. 2118.

Army Form C. 2118.

WAR DIARY
or
~~INTELLIGENCE SUMMARY~~.
(Erase heading not required.)

Instructions regarding War Diaries and Intelligence Summaries are contained in F. S. Regs., Part II. and the Staff Manual respectively. Title pages will be prepared in manuscript.

Headquarters RE 40th Division

Place	Date	Hour	Summary of Events and Information	Remarks and references to Appendices
CORBIE	1/2/17	10 pm	IInd Lt Rolfe RE 229th Fd Coy RE reports to CRE CORBIE with his section for Improvements to CORBIE Area	JD
—	2/2/17	10 pm	CRE CORBIE takes over charge of Saw Mill at AUBIGNY	JD
—	3/2/17	10 pm	Adjt proceeded to AMIENS to inspect the camouflage at Special Works Park there also the French camouflage	JD
—	4/2/17	10 pm	Routine work in office. Adjt proceeded to AUBIGNY to note progress at Saw Mill there.	JD
—	5/2/17	10 pm	CRE accompanies GOC in inspection of work progressing in Reserve area. Adjt proceeds to AUBIGNY to pay the 5 Sappers employed there	JD
—	6/2/17	10 pm	Routine Work.	JD
	7/2/17	10 pm	notified of the death of LceCpl Rolfe (106687) on the 5th inst at 21 CCS	JD
—	8/2/17	10 pm	CRE proceeded to PC BOMNET to take over from CRE 8th Division	JD
—	9/2/17	10 pm	Routine work in office. No 19827 Sgt Gordon + 105320 Sapper Marsden admitted to 21st CCS.	JD
	10/2/17	10 pm	Routine work and packing office for move on to PC BONNET	JD

2353 Wt. W2544/1454 700,000 5/15 D. D. & L. A.D.S.S./Forms/C. 2118.

Army Form C. 2118.

Instructions regarding War Diaries and Intelligence Summaries are contained in F. S. Regs., Part II. and the Staff Manual respectively. Title pages will be prepared in manuscript.

WAR DIARY
or
~~INTELLIGENCE SUMMARY.~~
(Erase heading not required.)

Headquarters RE 40th Division

Place	Date	Hour	Summary of Events and Information	Remarks and references to Appendices
PC BONNET	11/2/17	10pm	Headquarters RE move off from CORBIE to take up quarters at PC BONNET. Transport moved off 9 am under Lieut Cairns, & office staff at 9.30 with Adjutant, CRE at 10% CRE takes over work in RANCOURT Sector and DOMINO DUMP	JD
" "	12/2/17	10pm	Routine work	JD
" "	13/2/17			
" "	14/2/17			
" "	15/2/17	10pm	CE XV Corps visited 40th Division Area [illegible] with Major Ormiston. Lieut Cairns proceeded to 119th Infantry Brigade to take over duties of Bde Major temporarily	JD
" "	16/2/17	10pm	Routine work.	JD
" "	17/2/17	10pm	Routine work Sapper Marsden No 105320 returns from No 21 CCS	JD
" "	18/2/17	10pm	Routine work.	JD
" "	19/2/17	10pm	CE XV Corps visited CRE	JD
	20/2/17		Routine work.	JD
	21/2/17			
	22/2/17		Major Ormiston & Major Johnson visited CRE	JD
	23/2/17		Routine work.	JD
	24/2/17		CRE attends Corps Conference at PC CHAPEAU	JD

2353 Wt. W514/1454 700,000 5/15 D. D. & L. A.D.S.S./Forms/C. 2118.

Army Form C. 2118.

WAR DIARY
or
INTELLIGENCE ~~SUMMARY~~.
(Erase heading not required.)

Instructions regarding War Diaries and Intelligence Summaries are contained in F. S. Regs., Part II. and the Staff Manual respectively. Title pages will be prepared in manuscript.

Headquarters RE — 40th Division

Place	Date	Hour	Summary of Events and Information	Remarks and references to Appendices
PC BONNET	25/2/17	10pm	Major JOHNSON VC 231st (Field) Coy RE called on CRE to report progress on the new support line	JD
" "	26/2/17		CRE visited PC JEAN and PC CHAPEAU to see CRE 33rd Division and CRE 8th Division preparatory to taking over from 33rd Division	JD
" "	27/2/17	10pm	CRE proceeded with Col Walker to inspect the line held by the 33rd Division preparatory to taking over that area	JD
" "	28/2/17	10pm	Major Miller (224th Fd Coy RE) visited CRE to discuss his taking over arrangements	JD

Frank S ... Lieut RE
Adjt 40th DE
for CRE 40th Division

Instructions regarding War Diaries and Intelligence Summaries are contained in F. S. Regs., Part II. and the Staff Manual respectively. Title pages will be prepared in manuscript.

Army Form C. 2118.

WAR DIARY or INTELLIGENCE SUMMARY.

(Erase heading not required.)

HEAD QUARTERS 40th DIVISIONAL ENGINEERS. MARCH 1917. (1)

Place	Date	Hour	MAP. FRANCE Sheet 62c — Summary of Events and Information	Remarks and references to Appendices
PC BONNET	1/3/17	10pm	Routine work.	[illegible]
	2/3/17	–	CE XV Corps (Brig Genl Marshall) visited CRE reference the S Sound ranging section 4th Field Survey Coy RE's dugout accommodation NISSEN HUTS suggested as a temporary measure & matter referred to higher authority for consent, matter left pending decision —	[illegible]
"	3/3/17	"	Routine work. arrangements made by CRE to commence laying the 40 cm track & Infantry pontoon under Pioneer Officer to start 4-3-17 —	[illegible]
"	4/3/17	"	owing to operations undertaken against enemy by the division on our right it is decided to concentrate on the 40 cm track between B23a & Andover & about 500 yards is lifted	[illegible]
	5/3/17		Adjt proceeded to PC JEAN to make preliminary arrangements about taking over	[illegible]
	6/3/17	–	CRE attended Corps conference at PC CHAPEAU. arrangements made with CRE 8th Division & CRE 33rd Division for HQRE to move to new area on 8th inst	[illegible]
"	7/3/17	.	CRE proceeded to PC JEAN to prepare for taking over from 33rd Division —	[illegible]
PC JEAN H.1.c.4.9.	8/3/17	"	Head Quarters move to P.C. JEAN. CRE takes over from CRE 33rd Div. CRE 8th Div takes over work in RANCOURT SECTOR from CRE 40th Div. 40th Div. new front consists of CLERY SECTOR & BETHUNE Rd. Sector. Length of front 5700 yds. LOWLAND DUMP becomes 40th Div. main dump. Dumps at FRISE also taken over.	CBR.
	9.3.17.		Routine work.	CBR.

2353 Wt. W2544/1454 700,000 5/15 D. D. & L. A.D.S.S./Forms/C. 2118.

Instructions regarding War Diaries and Intelligence Summaries are contained in F. S. Regs., Part II. and the Staff Manual respectively. Title pages will be prepared in manuscript.

WAR DIARY
or
~~INTELLIGENCE SUMMARY.~~

Army Form C. 2118.

HEAD QUARTERS 40TH DIVISIONAL ENGINEERS (Erase heading not required.) MARCH 1917. (2)

Place	Date	Hour	Summary of Events and Information	Remarks and references to Appendices
P.C. JEAN.	10.3.17.		Routine work	ABR.
"	11.3.17		Routine work.	ABR.
"	12.3.17		Routine work.	ABR.
"	13.3.17		Routine work. LIEUT. F. DENTON admitted to hospital & sent to Corps Rest Station. CAPT. A.B. RAYMER assumes duties of Adjutant.	ABR.
"	14.3.17.		Routine work.	ABR.
"	15.3.17		Routine work. Special Stores obtained for possible advance	ABR.
"	16.3.17		Routine work do do	ABR.
"	17.3.17.		— do — Enemy retire from their position	ABR.
"	18.3.17.		— do — Work of Companies concentrated on roads to PERONNE & HAUT ALLAIN.	
"	19.3.17.		— do — do do Water Supply Special road & river reconnaissances prepared. Special Stores obtained	ABR
"	20.3.17		Routine work. Work of Companies as above. Special reconnaissance on Water Supply of HAUT ALLAINES and MT. ST. QUENTIN. MT ST QUENTIN – HAUT-ALLAINES defensive line held. 2 Companies assisting to consolidate this line.	
"	21.3.17		Routine work. Work of Companies as on 20th	ABR
"	22.3.17.		Routine work. Field Companies move forward with Brigades.	ABR.
"	23.3.17		Routine work "Lieut E. Wilburn assumes duties of Adjutant Major (Tem Lieut Col A.C. BAYLAY DSO RE reported for duty	EW
"	24.3.17.		Routine work. Work of Companies concentrated on Roads & assisting to consolidate Line of Resistance. Lieut Col A.C. BAYLAY visited all Companies	EW
"	25.3.17		Lt Col R.J.B. Mair RE proceeded to 6th Corp. Major (Tem Lieut Col A.C. Baylay assumed Command 40th Divl Engineers 23.3.17 C.R.E met C.E. XVth Corps & made a tour of the Roads in Area	EW
"	26.3.17		Routine Work. Work of Companies Concentrated on Roads one Company Bridge & Railway work. Capt H.P.B. Gough 17th Welsh Regt reported for 10 days instruction under C.R.E.	EW
"	27.3.17		Routine Work Work of Companies as on 26th. Mangle Dump becomes Divisional Dump "Lt H.R. Ruggles Brice H.Q.M. 40th DW reported for instruction under CRE	EW

2353 Wt. W2544/1454. 700,000 5/15 D. D. & L. A.D.S.S./Forms/C. 2118.

Army Form C. 2118.

Instructions regarding War Diaries and Intelligence Summaries are contained in F. S. Regs., Part II. and the Staff Manual respectively. Title pages will be prepared in manuscript.

WAR DIARY
or
~~INTELLIGENCE SUMMARY.~~
(Erase heading not required.)

HEAD QUARTERS
40th DIVISIONAL ENGINEERS

MARCH 1917

Place	Date	Hour	Summary of Events and Information	Remarks and references to Appendices
P.C. JEAN	28.3.17		Routine work — work of Companies same as 27th	EW
— —	29.3.17		do — do	EW
— —	30.3.17		do — do	EW
— —	31.3.17		do — do — 40th Div. Warning Order received	EW

E.Welburn Lieut RE
for Adj RE 40th Division

2353 Wt. W2544/1454 700,000 5/15 D. D. & L. A.D.S.S./Forms/C. 2118.

Army Form C. 2118.

WAR DIARY
or
~~INTELLIGENCE~~ SUMMARY.

(Erase heading not required.)

Instructions regarding War Diaries and Intelligence Summaries are contained in F. S. Regs., Part II. and the Staff Manual respectively. Title pages will be prepared in manuscript.

HQ RE — 40th Division — April 1917

Place	Date	Hour	Summary of Events and Information	Remarks and references to Appendices
PC JEAN	1/4/17	10pm	LIEUT F DENTON returned from Corps Rest Station and resumed duties of Adjutant	FD
	2/4/17 3/4/17 4/4/17 5/4/17		Supervision of road repairs in 40th Divisional Area CLERY – BOUCHAVESNES	FD
MANAN COURT	6/4/17		CRE's Headquarters move to MANANCOURT V 13 C 6.0	FD
"	7/4/17		2 Lieut L E WILBURN returned to 231st (Field) Coy RE. Instructions issued to 231st Fd Coy to bridge Canal du NORD at V8 b 2.7 (57c 1/40000) to take horsed traffic as ordered by XV Corps. Strength HQ O 2 OR 7. Attached O 1 OR 10	FD
	8/4/17 9/4/17		Supervision of work of Coys as follows 224th Fd Coy working with Infantry Brigade in line (121st) 231st ~~Field~~ Coy working on bridge at ETRICOURT and siting YTRES – SOREL line of defence	FD
	10/4/17		Bridge at ETRICOURT (V8 b 2.7) reported ready to take horsed transport XV Corps order same to be strengthened to take 3 ton lorries	FD
	11/4/17 12/4/17		work as 10/4/17	FD
	13/4/17		Bridge at ETRICOURT completed to carry 3 ton lorries	FD

2353 Wt. W2544/1454 700,000 5/15 D. D. & L. A.D.S.S./Forms/C. 2118.

Army Form C. 2118.

Instructions regarding War Diaries and Intelligence Summaries are contained in F. S. Regs., Part II. and the Staff Manual respectively. Title pages will be prepared in manuscript.

WAR DIARY
or
~~INTELLIGENCE~~ SUMMARY.
(Erase heading not required.)

HQ RE — 40th Division — April 1917

Place	Date	Hour	Summary of Events and Information	Remarks and references to Appendices
MANAN COURT	14/4/17, 15/4/17		Supervision of construction of Strong points on main line of resistance Q35a Q29C + a Q22 d + C Pioneers (12th Yorks Regt) repairing roads ETRICOURT - EQUANCOURT - FINS. YTRES - SOREL CONTINUED	
			Strength O2 OR6 attached O1 OR9	JD
	16/4/17		HQ 229th Fd Coy RE + 2 sections move to EQUANCOURT to work on main line resistance	JD
	17/4/17, 18/4/17, 19/4/17, 20/4/17, 21/4/17		Work + supervision as before	JD
	22/4/17		224th Fd Coy RE ordered to make forward dumps for consolidation after attack on BEAUCAMP + VILLERS PLUICH	JD
			STRENGTH O2 OR6 attached O1 OR9	JD
	23/4/17, 24/4/17		RE preparations for attack on BEAUCAMP + VILLERS PLUICH by 119th + 120th Infantry Brigades 224th Fd Coy attached 119th Bgde 229th attached 120th Bgde	JD
	25/4/17		229th Fd Coy ordered to search BEAUCAMP + VILLERS PLUICH captured for mines Pioneers ordered to dig CT Q23C to old German front LINK Q18d	JD

2353 Wt. W2544/1454 700,000 5/15 D. D. & L. A.D.S.S./Forms/C. 2118.

Instructions regarding War Diaries and Intelligence Summaries are contained in F. S. Regs., Part II. and the Staff Manual respectively. Title pages will be prepared in manuscript.

WAR DIARY
or
~~INTELLIGENCE SUMMARY~~.
(Erase heading not required.)

Army Form C. 2118.

HQ RE 40th Division April 1917

Place	Date	Hour	Summary of Events and Information	Remarks and references to Appendices
MAIVAN COURT	26/4/17		178th Tunnelling Coy place 2 officers + 110 OR under CRE's instructions for work on MGEs, wells + to make forward accommodation for HQ Brigades + artillery	JD
	27/4/17		231st Field Coy instructed to arrange the fixing of accommodation of S sound ranging section 4th Fd Survey Coy RE at Q35 b 6.0	JD
	28/4/17		Wiring + defence of new front organised Q11 b - Q12 central - R7 c + d - R8 c 5.0 - R14 b 3.3 - R14 d 0.0 - R21 c 4.0 Pioneers ordered to complete old main line of resistance to provide second line. Work on YTRES - SOREL line stopped	JD
	29/4/17		Division front to be held by 3 Infantry Brigades in line construction of advanced HQ for 121st Bgde also dugouts for 119th Bgde ordered at W4 a 0 4 Strength O2 OR6 attached O1 OR9	JD
	30/4/17		CRE holds conference of Coy (Field) Commanders & ordered Coys to be affiliated to Infantry Brigades for work as follows. 224th (Fd) Coy RE to 120th Bgde, 231st Fd Coy RE to 121st Bgde. Two to 119th Brigade, 229th Fd Coy RE attached to Dival RFA for dugout work at Batteries — parties of 1 NCO + 9 men	JD

Frank A. Sutton Capt RE
adj 40th DE

Instructions regarding War Diaries and Intelligence Summaries are contained in F. S. Regs., Part II. and the Staff Manual respectively. Title pages will be prepared in manuscript.

WAR DIARY
or
~~INTELLIGENCE~~ SUMMARY.
(Erase heading not required.)

Army Form C. 2118.

HQ RE — 40th Division — May 1917

Place	Date	Hour	Summary of Events and Information	Remarks and references to Appendices
MANAN COURT	1/5/17	10/0	Work on Infantry Brigade dugouts commenced by 178th Tunnelling Coy RE at Q23 c 5.3, Q29 a 8.6 Q29 b 1.3	[illegible]
"	2/5/17	10/16	Companies ordered to complete wiring of front + intermediate line by 5th inst + to make forward dumps of wire + pickets for consolidation after coming offensive against LA VACQUERIE	[illegible]
"	3/5/17	10/pm	Machine Gun defences of intermediate line arranged with MGO XV Corps	[illegible]
"	4/5/17	10.30	Orders given to 224th + 231st Field Companies to cancel arrangements for consolidating LA VACQUERIE after attack, orders having been received that LA VACQUERIE should be evacuated after destruction. Coys ordered to form demolition parties, two to each Brigade, for destruction of buildings, cellars + emplacements	[illegible]
"	5/5/17	10/30	Reconnaissance for cross country tracks to relieve traffic on roads. Birds-eye view photographs of LA VACQUERIE obtained for O.C. Demolition parties State O 2 OR 6 attached O 1 OR 9	[illegible]

2353 Wt. W2544/1454 700,000 5/15 D. D. & L. A.D.S.S./Forms/C. 2118.

Instructions regarding War Diaries and Intelligence Summaries are contained in F. S. Regs., Part II. and the Staff Manual respectively. Title pages will be prepared in manuscript.

WAR DIARY

or

~~INTELLIGENCE~~ SUMMARY.

HQ RE (*Erase heading not required.*) 40th Division

Army Form C. 2118.

1

Place	Date	Hour	Summary of Events and Information	Remarks and references to Appendices
MANAN COURT	6/4/17	10.0	Big raid on LA VACQUERIE on night 5/6th by 119th Infantry Brigade & 121st Infantry Brigade. Two Demolition Parties, each of 1 officer, 10 sappers, 20 Infantry carrying to accompany each Brigade appear to have been suitable parties. Their orders were to follow the Infantry moppers up and demolish houses cellars emplacements, dugouts in defined areas for each party. They carried cutting tools & hammers, 20 prepared 7 lb. GC charges and a number of P Bombs. The Left Brigade having failed to get through the village the two parties with that Bgde were unable to carry out their task. The parties with the Right Bgde however did a considerable amount of destruction to houses & dugouts. They had a very short time for the work owing to the final objectives being attained only 5 minutes before the set time to retire & they tried to carry on before the mopping up was completed with the result that they were interfered with a good deal by rifle fire & bombs from buildings	

2353 Wt. W2544/1454 700,000 5/15 D. D. & L. A.D.S.S./Forms/C. 2118.

Army Form C. 2118.

Instructions regarding War Diaries and Intelligence Summaries are contained in F. S. Regs., Part II, and the Staff Manual respectively. Title pages will be prepared in manuscript.

WAR DIARY
or
~~INTELLIGENCE SUMMARY~~.
(Erase heading not required.)

HQ RE 40th Division

Place	Date	Hour	Summary of Events and Information	Remarks and references to Appendices
MANAN COURT	7/5/17	10/30	Re sited Brown Line MAP 57c Q35c – Q21b with GSO 1 and detailed new work on same to Field Companies. Detailed work on Batt[n] HQ for 3 Brigade in line to 178th Tunnelling Coy RE	
"	8/5/17	10/30	Conference with O.C. Field Coys "Reconstruction of Brown Line"	
"	9/5/17	10/30	Conference at XV Corps HQ and orders given to make a proper defensive position with communication trenches etc	
"	10/5/17	11.0 pm	Orders received for Left Bgde to be relieved by Bgde of 20th Division on night 12/13 & Centre Bgde on night 13/14. Arranged for Pioneers to complete cutting through present front trench of Left Bgde. Orders given for 229th Fd Coy RE to take over from 490 (HC) Fd Coy RE & to move to HEUDICOURT on 12th inst. 231st Fd Coy RE to take over from 2nd Fd Coy RE & move to HEUDICOURT on 13th inst	
"	11/5/17	10/30	Taking over from CRE 8th Division arranged for. Pioneers to dig front line of Centre Bgde through	
"	12/5/17	10.30	229th Fd Coy RE moved to HEUDICOURT. Arrangements made for constructing [?] standings & new water points	

Army Form C. 2118.

Instructions regarding War Diaries and Intelligence Summaries are contained in F. S. Regs., Part II. and the Staff Manual respectively. Title pages will be prepared in manuscript.

WAR DIARY
or
~~INTELLIGENCE~~ SUMMARY.
(Erase heading not required.)

HQ RE 40th Division

Place	Date	Hour	Summary of Events and Information	Remarks and references to Appendices
MANAN COURT	13/5/17	10/30	231st Field Coy RE moved to HEUDICOURT	JD
"	14/5/17	10/-	Routine work	JD
"	15/5/17	10/30		
"	16/5/17	10/30	Routine work.	JD
"	17/5/17	10/0	MEUNIER Switch commenced.	JD
"	18/5/17	11/0	Routine	JD
"	19/5/17	11/0	Sited Switch to SE from X17b – X16d (map 57c) and work commenced	JD
"	20/5/17	10/0	Routine	JD
"	21/5/17	11/0	Handing over work + shewing ground to CRE 35th Division	JD
"	22/5/17	10/30	Conference of Coy Commanders arranging moves + future work	JD
"	23/5/17	11/0	Sited GOUZEAUCOURT SWITCH	JD
"	24/5/17	10/0	Conference at XV Corps Headquarters	JD
"	25/5/17	11/0	Sited Strongpoint at QUENTIN MILL	JD

Army Form C. 2118.

Instructions regarding War Diaries and Intelligence Summaries are contained in F. S. Regs., Part II. and the Staff Manual respectively. Title pages will be prepared in manuscript.

WAR DIARY
or
~~INTELLIGENCE SUMMARY~~.

HQ RE (*Erase heading not required.*) 40th Division

Place	Date	Hour	Summary of Events and Information	Remarks and references to Appendices
MANAN COURT	26/5/17	10/pm	CRE issued outline of work to be done by Field Coys, Pioneers & Tunnelling Coy Sections in making defensive position & accommodation for troops forward	JD
"	27/5/17	10/pm	CRE left for FLIXECOURT to attend 4th Army School	JD
"	28/5/17 29/5/17 30/5/17 31/5/17		Routine work	JD

Frank D... Capt RE
for CRE 40th Division

2353 Wt. W2544/1454 700,000 5/15 D. D. & L. A.D.S.S./Forms/C. 2118.

Instructions regarding War Diaries and Intelligence Summaries are contained in F. S. Regs., Part II. and the Staff Manual respectively. Title pages will be prepared in manuscript.

WAR DIARY
or
~~INTELLIGENCE~~ SUMMARY.

(*Erase heading not required.*)

Army Form C. 2118.

Place	Date	Hour	Summary of Events and Information	Remarks and references to Appendices
MANANCOURT	1/6/17 – 6/6/17		Routine work	FD
	7/6/17		CRE returns from Senior Officers Conference	FD
	8/6/17 – 10/6/17		Routine	FD
	11/6/17		Conference of Coy Commanders at 229th Fd Coy RE HQ	FD
	12/6/17 – 14/6/17		Routine inspecting work in progress on Divisional area	FD
	15/6/17 – 21/6/17		Routine	FD
	22/6/17 – 25/6/17		Schemes of defence & accommodation in Divisional Area and preparation of area for offensive operations	FD
	26/6/17 – 28/6/17		Arranging to take over 35th Division RE work marking out III Corps camping sites. Arranging for new 40th Division Headquarters to be constructed at SOREL V18 d 5.7	FD
	29/6/17 – 30/6/17		CRE proceeded on leave 29-6-17	FD

Frank Dent ? Capt RE
for CRE 40th Division

Instructions regarding War Diaries and Intelligence Summaries are contained in F. S. Regs., Part II. and the Staff Manual respectively. Title Pages will be prepared in manuscript.

WAR DIARY
or
~~INTELLIGENCE SUMMARY~~
(Erase heading not required.)

Army Form C. 2118

HQ RE — 40th Division

Place	Date	Hour	Summary of Events and Information	Remarks and references to Appendices
MANAN COURT	1/7/17	10am	Work commenced on new Divisional HQ at site selected at SOREL W18d 5.7. State strength 1 Off 5 OR attached 1 Off 7 OR	JD
"	2/7/17 to 5/7/17		Supervision of camp schemes in 40th Division being marked & the erection of the DHQ	JD
SOREL	6/7/17		Headquarters move to SOREL	JD
"	7/7/17			
"	8/7/17		Routine & supervision of work in hand.	JD
"	9/7/17			
"	10/7/17		Strength 8th 1 Off 5 OR attached 1 Off 8 OR	
"	11/7/17		CRE returns from leave	JD
"	12/7/17 to 16/7/17		Supervision of defensive position works improvement of communications and accommodation of troops	JD
			Strength 15th 2 Off 5 OR attached 1 Off 8 OR.	
"	17/7/17		Laid out retarded support line in Right Brigade Sector	JD
"	18/7/17		Laid out Reserve Line at Welch Ridge VILLERS PLOUICH	JD

Instructions regarding War Diaries and Intelligence Summaries are contained in F. S. Regs., Part II. and the Staff Manual respectively. Title Pages will be prepared in manuscript.

WAR DIARY
or
~~INTELLIGENCE SUMMARY~~
(Erase heading not required.)

Army Form C. 2118

HQ RE 40th DIV

Place	Date	Hour	Summary of Events and Information	Remarks and references to Appendices
SOREL	19/7/17		Demonstration of Bangalore Torpedoes to CE XIth French Corps. Support line between Strar Avenue & Leith Walk started –	HRRD
	20/7/17		Commenced work in repairing Gouzeaucourt – Villers Guislain road & filling of Craters –	HRRD
	21/7/17		Alteration in Water Supply scheme by which Twenty two ravine is supplied from Gonnelieu instead of from Villers Guislain.	HRRD
	22/7/17		New reserve line by Villers Plouich started –	HRRD
	23/7/17 to 27/7/17		Rye plates used for first time for OP, put up in Gonnelieu. Supervision of work in hand –	HRRD
	28/7/17		Inspection of Gun Emplacements as to protection against 5.9" shell –	HRRD
	29/7/17		Conference of OC's Coys – Arranged for Coys making further Winter Camps – Made disposition for Coys & Works Coys attached in case of attack. Villers Plouich Reserve line completed –	HRRD
	30/7/17		Prospecting of sites for winter camps for two battalions –	HARRIS
	31/7/17		Siting new MG Emplacements in front system with Divisional MG Officer	HARRIS

HRRugsley-Davis 2nd Lieut RE
for CRE 40 Division

1875 Wt. W593/826 1,000,000 4/15 J.B.C. & A. A.D.S.S./Forms/C. 2118.

Instructions regarding War Diaries and Intelligence Summaries are contained in F. S. Regs., Part II. and the Staff Manual respectively. Title Pages will be prepared in manuscript.

WAR DIARY
or
INTELLIGENCE SUMMARY
(Erase heading not required.)

Army Form C. 2118

Place	Date	Hour	Summary of Events and Information	Remarks and references to Appendices
SOREL	1/8/17		Readjustment of front taking over on left to Q5d92 Sheet 57c SE 1/20000 from 9th division & handing over on right Sunken road X11.c06 to 35th division –	HRRB
	2/8/17		Conference of OC's Companies –	
	3/8/17		Tour of front line taken over from 9th Division (Beaucamp area) by CRE –	HRRB
	4/8/17 5/8/17		Supervision of work in hand –	HRRB
	6/8/17		Sitting of dugouts for Coy Hqrs left sector –	HRRB
	7/8/17 8/8/17 9/8/17 10/8/17		Supervision of work in hand Adj rejoins from leave 8-8-17 Major Skipworth attached CRE for instruction	[illegible]
	12/8/17		CRE gives a lecture on RE to IIIrd Corps school FOUCAUCOURT	[illegible]
	13/8/17 14/8/17 17/8/17		Routine & supervision	

1875 Wt. W593/826 1,000,000 4/15 J.B.C. & A. A.D.S.S./Forms/C. 2118.

Instructions regarding War Diaries and Intelligence Summaries are contained in F. S. Regs., Part II. and the Staff Manual respectively. Title Pages will be prepared in manuscript.

WAR DIARY
or
INTELLIGENCE SUMMARY
(Erase heading not required.)

Army Form C. 2118

Place	Date	Hour	Summary of Events and Information	Remarks and references to Appendices
SOREL LE GRAND	18/8/17 – 19/8/17		} Routine State O 2 OR 6 attached O 2 OR 9	[initials]
	20/8/17 – 26/8/17		} Supervision & routine 2Lt HR Ruggles-Brise is attached to Major General Ponsonby Commanding 40th Div as ADC 25-8-17. Notification received that one Field Coy RE is to be withdrawn from the Division the 229th Fd Coy RE [illegible] State O 2 OR 6 attached O 2 OR 8	[initials]
	27/8/17		Reconnaissance of YTRES-SOREL Corps line from V6d0.3 sheet 57c SE to E4 62c NE	[initials]
	28/8/17 – 29/8/17		} Inspection of progress in winter Hutted camps	[initials]
	30/8/17		Major Skipwith returns to 35th Division	[initials]
	31/8/17		Routine	[initials]

Frank Dent Capt RE
for a/CRE 40th Division

1875 Wt. W593/826 1,000,000 4/15 J.B.C. & A. A.D.S.S./Forms/C. 2118.

Instructions regarding War Diaries and Intelligence Summaries are contained in F. S. Regs., Part II. and the Staff Manual respectively. Title Pages will be prepared in manuscript.

WAR DIARY
or
INTELLIGENCE SUMMARY
(Erase heading not required.)

Army Form C. 2118

HQ 40th Division Engineers

Place	Date	Hour	Summary of Events and Information	Remarks and references to Appendices
SOREL LEGRAND	1/9/17		Routine	
"	2/9/17		State 2 Off 10 OR attached - Off 6 OR	[illegible]
	7/9/17 8/9/17		CRE attends conference at 119th Bgde HQ 7-9-17	[illegible]
	9/9/17		State 2 Off 10 OR attached 6 OR	[illegible]
	10/9/17 13/9/17		Supervision of work in forward and back areas	[illegible]
	14/9/17		CRE attends conference to discuss scheme of tunnels for offence and defence	[illegible]
	15/9/17		CRE & Major Baltye discuss scheme on site	[illegible]
	16/9/17 17/9/17		Routine State 16-9-17 2 Off 10 OR attached 20 Off 7 OR	[illegible]
	18/9/17		Experiments carried out at DHQ with life size camouflage figures procured from Special Works Park AMIENS with a view to employing	

1875 Wt. W593/826 1,000,000 4/15 J.B.C. & A. A.D.S.S./Forms/C. 2118.

Instructions regarding War Diaries and Intelligence Summaries are contained in F. S. Regs., Part II. and the Staff Manual respectively. Title Pages will be prepared in manuscript.

WAR DIARY
or
INTELLIGENCE SUMMARY
(Erase heading not required.)

Army Form C. 2118

Place	Date	Hour	Summary of Events and Information	Remarks and references to Appendices
			them to bring down enemy barrage by disclosing point of apparent attack. The method used was to hinge the figures, by means of a batten + French wire staples, to the ground placing immediately behind the figure a long screw picket with a pronounced forward inclination + raise or lower the figure by means of a wire passing through the ring at top of screw picket + thence through other screw pickets to the trench where it was operated. The dummies should be placed if possible a good hundred yards in advance of our trench. It was found best to operate in groups of three + necessary to weight the head of the figure to enable it to fall when released. This method was employed with success by the 231st Fd. Coy RE on the night 22nd Sept 1917 in a raid forward of BEAUCAMP in which the raiding party took 10 prisoners with very slight casualties	
	9/9/17		Routine	JD
	23/9/17		Major WE Kidner 40th Divisional Signal Coy RE proceeded to report to War Office for duty 21-9-17. State 23-9-17 2 off 100 OR att 1 off 7 OR	JD
	24/9/17		Major EW Ormiston handed over the command of 229th Fd Coy to Capt JW Clark (231st Fd Coy RE) + proceeded to England to report for duty	JD

1875 Wt. W593/826 1,000,000 4/15 J.B.C. & A. A.D.S.S./Forms/C. 2118.

Instructions regarding War Diaries and Intelligence Summaries are contained in F. S. Regs., Part II. and the Staff Manual respectively. Title Pages will be prepared in manuscript.

WAR DIARY
or
~~INTELLIGENCE SUMMARY~~

(Erase heading not required.)

Army Form C. 2118

H Q R Engineers 40th Division

Place	Date	Hour	Summary of Events and Information	Remarks and references to Appendices
BOREL LE GRAND	25/9/17 to 30/9/17		Routine State on 30-9-17 2 off 10 OR attached 1 off 8 OR.	

Chamberlain Capt R.E.
Adjt 40th DE

1875 Wt. W593/826 1,000,000 4/15 J.B.C. & A. A.D.S.S./Forms/C. 2118.

Instructions regarding War Diaries and Intelligence Summaries are contained in F. S. Regs., Part II. and the Staff Manual respectively. Title Pages will be prepared in manuscript.

WAR DIARY
or
~~INTELLIGENCE SUMMARY~~

Army Form C. 2118

Headquarters 40th (Erase heading not required.) Divisional Engineers

Place	Date	Hour	Summary of Events and Information	Remarks and references to Appendices
SOREL LE GRAND	1/10/17 – 4/10/17		Routine	HRR-B
	5/10/17		231st Field Coy ~~RE~~ relieved in ~~Beaucamp~~ - Villers Plouich Sector by 83rd Fd Coy RE and moved to Camp W20 near Dessart Wood –	HRR-B
	6/10/17 – 7/10/17		Routine 229th Field Coy relieved in Gouzeaucourt (Centre sector) by 96th Fd Coy RE – Staff O.2 OR 6 Attached O 2 OR 8.	HRR-B
	8/10/17		Routine	
	9/10/17		224th Fd Coy RE relieved in Villers Guislain (Right Bde Sector) by 84th Fd Coy RE and moved to new billets in Heudecourt.	HRR-B
	10/10/17		HQ 40th Div Engineers moved to Heudecourt from Sorel on completion of relief by 20th Div –	HRR-B
			Lt Col AH Becher 12th Yorks (Pioneers) assumed temporary duties of CRE during absence of Lt Col AC Bayley DSO on leave.	HRR-B
			Capt F Druton (~~[illegible]~~) assumed temporary command of 231 Fd Coy RE during 1 months absence of Major FH Johnson MC on leave.	HRR-B
	11/10/17		Routine :- i.e 224 Fd Coy RE erecting shelters near Gouzeaucourt in Sunken road. 231 . . . . repairing FINS – GOUZEAUCOURT RD by process of using Cement & fine slag (from old Rly) & road metal for concreting over the existing pavé	HRR-B
	12/10/17		Routine –	HRR-B

1875 Wt. W593/826 1,000,000 4/15 J.B.C. & A. A.D.S.S./Forms/C. 2118.

Instructions regarding War Diaries and Intelligence Summaries are contained in F. S. Regs., Part II. and the Staff Manual respectively. Title Pages will be prepared in manuscript.

Army Form C. 2118

WAR DIARY
or
~~INTELLIGENCE SUMMARY~~

Head Quarters 40th (Erase heading not required.) Divisional Engineers -

Place	Date	Hour	Summary of Events and Information	Remarks and references to Appendices
HEUDECOURT			Routine	
	13/10/17		State 2 officers 6 OR :- att^d 2 officers 8 OR -	(HRRA)
	14/10/17		"	
	15/10/17		"	
	16/10/17		"	
	17/10/17			
PERONNE	18/10/17		HQ 40th Div RE, 224 Fd Coy RE, 231 Fd Coy RE moved by decauville, transport by road, to Peronne.	(HRRA)
FOSSEUX	19/10/17		HQ 40th Div RE, 224 Fd Coy RE, 231 Fd Coy RE personnel rejoined 40th Division by train. HQ 40th Div RE opened at Fosseux - Transport of above moved by road to Bapaume area -	(HRRA)
	20/10/17		Transport of HQ 40th Div RE moved from Bapaume area to Fosseux, of Field Coys to new divisional area	
	21/10/17		Lt Col HC Bayley CRE 40th Div returned from leave its England. Division in rest - State :- 2 off, 6 OR. att^d 7 OR	(HRRA)
	22/10/17		Division in rest billets -	
	23/10/17		"	
	24/10/17		"	
	25/10/17			
	26/10/17		"	
	27/10/17		"	(HRRA)
	28/10/17		Transport of HQ 40th RE, HQ & ½ 224, 229, 231 Field Coys RE and 12th Yorks (Pioneers) marched to Bapaume Area. State 2 off, 6 OR. Att^d 7 OR	
PERONNE	29/10/17		" " HQ 40th Div RE, HQ & ½ 224 & 231 " & 12th Yorks " from " " to Peronne, 229 to Moislains. Personnel of above & 12th Yorks (Pioneers) by train to Peronne for work under CE IIIrd Corps. Personnel of 229 Fd Coy RE & 12th Yorks marched from Peronne to Moislains -	(HRRA)

1875 Wt. W593/826 1,000,000 4/15 J.B.C. & A. A.D.S.S./Forms/C. 2118.

Army Form C. 2118

WAR DIARY
or
~~INTELLIGENCE SUMMARY~~

Instructions regarding War Diaries and Intelligence Summaries are contained in F. S. Regs., Part II. and the Staff Manual respectively. Title Pages will be prepared in manuscript.

Headquarters 40th (Erase heading not required.) Divisional Engineers –

Place	Date	Hour	Summary of Events and Information	Remarks and references to Appendices
EQUANCOURT	30/10/17		HQ 40th Div RE, HQ & ½ 224 Fd Coy RE and 231 Fd Coy RE moved by road from Peronne to Equancourt.	HRR-B
	31/10/17		SORE IIIrd Corps came over and detailed work to be carried out by ½ 224 Fd Coy RE and 231 Fd Coy RE concerning the erection of shelters in and around FINS. 229 Fd Coy RE started work under CRE IIIrd Corps troops erecting shelters near Moislains. 12th Yorks Regt (Pioneers) started work under CRE IIIrd Corps troops working in conjunction with 229 Fd Coy RE.	HRR-B

H R Ruggles-Brise
Capt RE
Adjt 40th Div Engineers

HQ RE 40 D

Vol 18

H.Q.,
40TH DIVISIONAL
ENGINEERS.
No. 18
Date 1. 12. 17

Confidential

Vol. 18.

War Diaries

of

Headquarters R.E.

~~224 Field Co R.E.~~

~~229 Field Co R.E.~~

~~231 Field Co R.E.~~

Army Form C. 2118

Instructions regarding War Diaries and Intelligence Summaries are contained in F. S. Regs., Part II. and the Staff Manual respectively. Title Pages will be prepared in manuscript.

WAR DIARY
or
~~INTELLIGENCE SUMMARY~~

Headquarters 40th (Erase heading not required.) Divisional Engineers.

Place	Date	Hour	Summary of Events and Information	Remarks and references to Appendices
EQUANCOURT.	1/11/17		½ 224 Fd Coy RE and 231 Fd Coy RE started work in FINS, erecting shelters to provide accomodation for 2 Battns. – 229 Fd Coy RE & 12th Yorks Regt Pioneers continued work under CRE IIIrd Corps troops erecting shelters near Moislains –	HRRD
	2/11/17		C E IIIrd Corps visited Hqrs 40th Div RE.	HRRD
	3/11/17		Routine. ½ 224 Fd Coy RE completed work in FINS. State 2 off 6 OR AHd 7 OR 3 OR on leave.	HRRD
	4/11/17		½ 224 & 2 sections 231 Fd Coy RE started erection of shelters in EQUANCOURT.	HRRD
	5/11/17		Routine –	MRP
	6/11/17		Routine –. Capt Ruggles Brise R.E. granted 10 days leave to U.K.	MRP
	7/11/17		Routine –	MRP
	8/11/17		Routine. C.R.E attended Conference at 20th D.H.Q. – SOREL – 5.30 PM.	MRP
	9/11/17		Routine – Party of Officer + 100 OR of the 12 YORKS (Pioneers) reported FINS DUMP	MRP
	10/11/17		Routine – STATE – 16 off + 60 O.R. + 6 attached	MRP
	11/11/17		Routine	MRP
	12/11/17		Routine.	MRP
	13/11/17		Routine – C.R.E granted leave to PARIS –. Major Johnson V.C. R.E returned from leave, + acting C.R.E.	MRP
	14/11/17		Routine. –	MRP
	15/11/17		Routine – 1 Platoon – 12 YORKS (Pioneers) reported FINS DUMP. a/CRE attended C.E's conference at 20th D.H.Q – SOREL – 5-30 PM. 40th Divn (less RFA + RE) moved into V CORPS Area	MRP

Instructions regarding War Diaries and Intelligence Summaries are contained in F. S. Regs., Part II. and the Staff Manual respectively. Title pages will be prepared in manuscript.

WAR DIARY
or
INTELLIGENCE SUMMARY.

(*Erase heading not required.*) Headquarters 40th Divisional Engineers.

Army Form C. 2118.

Place	Date	Hour	Summary of Events and Information	Remarks and references to Appendices
EQUANCOURT.	16/11/17		Routine.	[illegible]
	17/11/17		Routine CE. 5th CORPS ~~visited the Office~~ came to see CRE. State 6. OR attached 6 OR. On leave 2 off. 3 OR.	[illegible]
	18/11/17		Routine.	[illegible]
HAPLINCOURT	19/11/17		Routine. Divl. RE + Pioneers moved to Division in New Area. HQ 40th Div RE rejoined Divl HQ at Haplincourt. 224 Fd Coy RE moved to Rocquigny. 229 Barastre. 231 Beaulencourt	[illegible]
	20/11/17		231st Field Coy RE & 12th Yorks Pioneers moved from Beaulencourt to Beaumetz-les Cambrai (2 sections of 231 Fd Coy RE for work under CRE 56 Div) remainder to repair road East of Demicourt to Canal du Nord. CRE attended conference at Div HQ. CE Vth Corps visited HQ 40th Div RE.	HRRB
BEAUMETZ-les-Cambrai	21/11/17		HQ 40th Div RE, 224, 229 Coys RE moved to Beaumetz-les-Cambrai & vicinity — 231 Fd Coy RE ~~Pioneers~~ & 12th Yorks employed on repair of above road. Section of 252 Tunnelling Coy placed at disposal of CRE for work, later placed at disposal of CRE 56th Div.	HRRB
HAVRINCOURT	22/11/17		Reconnaissance & work on cross country tracks East of Demicourt — 231 Fd Coy repairing bridge K9b for wheeled traffic. 40th Division transferred from Vth Corps to IVth Corps. HQ 40th Div RE ~~224 Fd Coy RE, 229~~ [struck through, illegible] moved from Beaumetz les Cambrai ~~& vicinity~~ to Havrincourt.	
	23/11/17		224, 229, 231 Field Coys RE & 12th Yorks Pioneers moved from Beaumetz les Cambrai & vicinity to Havrincourt	HRRB
	24/11/17		224 & 229 Fd Coy RE were sent up to reconnoitre & make strong points to retain objectives gained by 119 & 121 Inf Bdes at Bourlon Wood. 231 Fd Coy RE held in reserve. 12th Yorks Regt Pioneers worked on roads in & N of Havrincourt. Major T W D Miller RE 224 Fd Coy RE was wounded. State 2 off 4 OR — attached 7 OR.	HRRB HRRB

A5834 Wt. W4973/M687 750,000 8/16 D. D. & L. Ltd. Forms/C.2118/13.

Instructions regarding War Diaries and Intelligence Summaries are contained in F. S. Regs., Part II. and the Staff Manual respectively. Title Pages will be prepared in manuscript.

WAR DIARY
or
~~INTELLIGENCE SUMMARY~~
(Erase heading not required.)

Army Form C. 2118

Headquarters 40th Divisional Engineers

Place	Date	Hour	Summary of Events and Information	Remarks and references to Appendices
25/4/17	HAVRINCOURT		40th Div relieved by 62nd Div – Hqrs 40th Div RE, 224, 229, 231 Fd Coys RE and 12th Yorks Regt Pioneers remained at Havrincourt for work under 62nd Div – Conference of OC's units at which CRE detailed work to be carried out in connection with digging of new line through Bourlon Wood – 2 Coys of 12th Yorks Regt Pioneers to remain on roads –	HRRB
26/4/17	"		HQ 40th Div less Hqrs 40th Div RE moved to Neuville – Major F H Johnson VC 231 Field Coy RE was killed – 401 Fd Coy RE (51st Division) moved to Havrincourt for work under CRE 40th Div –	HRRB
27/4/17	"		401 Fd Coy RE started work on cross country tracks between Havrincourt & Graincourt. Continuation of digging & wiring new line through Bourlon Wood –	HRRB
28/4/17	"		ditto " " " } 40th Div congratulated by Commander in chief on their success. 47th Div relieved 62nd Div	HRRB
29/4/17	"		All Field Coys RE attached to 59th Div for work on roads North of Havrincourt & Flesquieres, 12th Yorks Regt Pioneers to 47th Div, also for roads & cross country tracks	HRRB
30/4/17	"		Enemy attacked West of Bourlon, also opposite Gonnelieu – Gouzeaucourt – Owing to uncertainty of position road work suspended by order of 47th Div & notice given that units should be prepared to evacuate Havrincourt – Lt Col A C Baylay DSO CRE 40th Div proceeded to RE School of Instruction Blendecques as Commandant. Lt Col H W Becher DSO 12 Yorks Regt (Pioneers) assumed duties of acting CRE.	HRRB

H R Ruggles-Brise Capt RE
for CRE 40th Div 30/4/17

1875 Wt. W593/826 1,000,000 4/15 J.B.C. & A. A.D.S.S./Forms/C. 2118.

Army Form C. 2118.

WAR DIARY
or
~~INTELLIGENCE SUMMARY.~~
(Erase heading not required.)

Instructions regarding War Diaries and Intelligence Summaries are contained in F. S. Regs., Part II. and the Staff Manual respectively. Title pages will be prepared in manuscript.

Headquarters 40th Div'l Engineers

Place	Date	Hour	Summary of Events and Information	Remarks and references to Appendices
HAVRINCOURT	1/12/17		Units continued work on Havrincourt - Flesquieres road - 12th Yorks Regt Pioneers on cross country tracks and roads in and from Havrincourt to GRAINCOURT. Lt Col G T P Goodwin RE appointed acting CRE vice Lt Col A C Bayley DSO RE temporarily detached as Commandant RE School of Instruction Blendecques.	HPR
	2/12/17		Routine	HPR
BEHAGNIES	3/12/17		Hqrs 40th Div Engineers rejoined DHQ at Behagnies (VI Corps area)	HPR
	4/12/17		T/Capt E L Martin 572 Field Coy RE assumed command of 224 Fd Coy RE vice A/Major T R D Miller RE wounded. 224, 229, 231 Fd Coys & 12th Yorks Regt Pioneers moved from Havrincourt to Bovry Becquerelle, St Leger, Hamelincourt, Boyelles respectively, (transport to Beaulencourt) to take over from 16th Div in the line. 2 Sections of 174 Tunnelling Coy RE placed at disposal of CRE for work. Letter of appreciation from GOC 62nd Div on work of RE & Pioneers in Bourlon Wood App I.	HPR

A5834 Wt. W4973/M687 750,000 8/16 D. D. & L. Ltd. Forms/C.2118/13.

Army Form C. 2118.

WAR DIARY
or
~~INTELLIGENCE SUMMARY.~~
(Erase heading not required.)

Instructions regarding War Diaries and Intelligence Summaries are contained in F. S. Regs., Part II. and the Staff Manual respectively. Title pages will be prepared in manuscript.

Hqrs 40th Divisional Engineers

Place	Date	Hour	Summary of Events and Information	Remarks and references to Appendices
BEHAGNIES	5/12/17		Transport of Field Coys proceeded from Beaulencourt to their respective destinations 224, 229, 231 Fd Coys RE to Boiry Becquerelle, St Leger, Hamelincourt respectively. Companies resting.	HRRJ
			Adjustment of Div'l boundaries. 40th Div No 1073/8G App II.	HRRJ
	6/12/17		Fd Coys started work on Intermediate Line & forward work in their respective Bde areas – State 2 off 6 OR. Attd 7 OR.	HRRJ
	7/12/17		Routine – Reserve Bde supplies daily working party of 400 off & OR for work on Intermediate Line	HRRJ
	8/12/17		" "	HRRJ
	9/12/17		" " – 1 Section 231 Fd Coy RE started work on new Stables & Garage at new DHQ Courcelette.	HRRJ
	10/12/17		" " 2 Sections 231 Fd Coy RE working as above. Special orders issued to Coys in event of hostile attack.	HRRJ
	11/12/17		" " CRE attended conference at 119 Inf Bde HQ (119 Inf Bde)	HRRJ
	12/12/17		In anticipation of attack by enemy Companies warned as to defensive positions to be occupied.	HRRJ

A5834 Wt. W4973/M687 750,000 8/16 D. D. & L. Ltd. Forms/C.2118/13.

Instructions regarding War Diaries and Intelligence Summaries are contained in F. S. Regs., Part II. and the Staff Manual respectively. Title pages will be prepared in manuscript.

WAR DIARY

or

~~INTELLIGENCE~~ SUMMARY.

(*Erase heading not required.*)

Army Form C. 2118.

Hqrs 40th Divisional Engineers

Place	Date	Hour	Summary of Events and Information	Remarks and references to Appendices
BEHAGNIES	13/12/17		Routine	HRRD
GOMIECOURT	14/12/17		HQ 40th Divisional Engineers moved to GOMIECOURT. – 1 Section 231 Fd Coy RE ceased work on new DHQ Gomiecourt, 1 Section remaining to complete the work.	HRRD
	15/12/17		229 Fd Coy RE took part in minor operation in conjunction with 119 Inf Bde against Neptune Trench, with view to destroying existing dugouts & supervising the digging of new trench to retain ground gained App III	
			State 2 off 5 OR attd 1 off 9 OR.	App III HRRD
	16, 17, 18		Routine	HRRD
	19		ditto – Appreciation of operation carried out by 119 Inf Bde (229 Fd Coy cooperating) App IV	App IV HRRD
	20		All field Coys ordered to concentrate on wiring for 3 days.	
	21		ditto	
	22		– – – – – – – State 2 off 5 OR attd 1 off 7 OR	HRRD
	23		1 Section 181 Tunnelling Coy RE attached for work	HRRD

A5834 Wt. W4973/M687 750,000 8/16 D. D. & L. Ltd. Forms/C.2118/13.

1918

DECEMBER

Army Form C. 2118.

WAR DIARY
or
INTELLIGENCE SUMMARY.
(Erase heading not required.)

Instructions regarding War Diaries and Intelligence Summaries are contained in F. S. Regs., Part II. and the Staff Manual respectively. Title pages will be prepared in manuscript.

Hqrs 40th

Place	Date	Hour	Summary of Events and Information	Remarks and references to Appendices
GOMIECOURT	24		Routine	HRR
	25		Xmas day – Companies at rest –	HRR
	26		Routine	HRR
	27		Readjustment of Div! front thereby handing over left sector to 3rd Div and taking over 3rd Div! area. 231 Fd Coy RE moved from HAMELINCOURT to MORY to take over from 529 Fd Coy RE in the line	HRR
	28		229 Fd Coy RE destroyed two abandoned enemy pillboxes in No Mans land. App V. 1 Section 181 Tunnelling Coy RE transferred (App V) – for work to CRE 34th Div.	HRR
	29		224 Fd Coy RE moved from Boiry Becquerelle and forward billets to Ervillers, forward sections to Boyelles to take over from 438 Fd Coy RE (3rd Div) in the line – Work in 224 & 231 Fd Coys late sector taken over by 34th Div – State 2 off 6 OR admitted 1 off 5 OR	HRR
	30		Routine – CRE attended conference HQ Alle HQ – Hutting & Stabling scheme for rear areas issued to Coys. 229 Fd Coy RE demolished an abandoned concrete MG emplacement and dug out	HRR (App VI)
	31		Routine	HRR

H R Russell Capt RE
for CRE 40th Div 31/12/17

A5834 Wt. W4973/M687 750,000 8/16 D. D. & L. Ltd. Forms/C.2118/13.

App I

1st. December, 1917.

Dear Ponsonby,

I must write you a line to tell you how splendidly your Sappers and Pioneers worked in BOURLON WOOD whilst attached to this Division.

They worked like Trojans, and the wiring of the main line of resistance and the Strong Point at the Cross Roads on the night 28th/29th was really a first class piece of work.

Bailey is undoubtedly a first class man. We are all very grateful to him and to his gallant men.

Yours sincerely,

(Sd) WALTER BRAITHWAITE,

War Diary

4.12.17

40th Div. No.1073/8.G   S E C R E T.

Appx II

C.R.A.   34th Division.
C.R.E.
121st Inf. Bde.
120th Inf. Bde.
119th Inf. Bde.

-*-*-*-*-*-*-*-*-*-

1. On the night 6th/7th Dec. the 121st Brigade will take over from the 34th Division that portion of the line properly belonging to the Centre Division, VI Corps, which has been temporarily held by the 34th Division since the night of November 18th/19th.

2. The dividing line between the 40th Division and the 34th Division will then run eastwards from the junction of BROWN Support with SHAFT AVENUE along SHAFT AVENUE and PUG AVENUE (both inclusive to 40th Division) to U.1.b.5.5.

3. Details will be arranged between Brigades concerned.

4. Acknowledge.

Major,
General Staff, 40th Division.

4th December, 1917.

War Diary

App III

RE War Diary

C.R.E. (for retention)

CONFIDENTIAL.

ON NO ACCOUNT TO BE TAKEN FURTHER FORWARD THAN BATTALION HEADQUARTERS

VI CORPS DAILY INTELLIGENCE SUMMARY NO. 635.
Issued December 15th, 1917. 8 p.m.

1. OPERATIONS.

VI Corps Front (6 p.m. 14th to 6 p.m. 15th December).

The attack by the enemy late yesterday afternoon was a half-hearted attempt on the northern side of BULLECOURT, which was easily repulsed. Only about 1 officer and 16 men came over the open, and quite half were shot down. A dead body was brought in, identifying the presence of the 16th Bavarian Division.

The night passed quietly on the whole front, and there was less artillery activity on both sides. We projected gas successfully on CHERISY.

The situation is unchanged on the right, and the day has been quieter than usual. Artillery on both sides has been intermittently active. The NOREUIL Ridge was shelled about noon.

At 3 p.m. the centre division raided the German trench between TRIDENT ALLEY, U.21.a 9.4, and VULCAN ALLEY, U.20.b 7.8, with the object of destroying the trench and dugouts, and of blowing up the Mebus NEPTUNE and PLUTO. The raid was successful and the objective was gained. Explosions are reported in the mebus. Two wounded prisoners were captured, one of whom has since died. Consolidation is in progress to improve our line between TRIDENT ALLEY and JOVE through MAGOG. The situation is quiet again.

On the left, the enemy retaliated with light trench mortars on our front line to a T.M. shoot, but no damage was caused. Between 1.15 and 2.30 p.m. the hostile artillery was active on the left sub-sector.

Hostile aircraft were active.

Our artillery fired on the APEX this morning, and between 12.30 and 2 p.m. carried out a concentrated shoot on it. A concentration of 2,800 rounds was fired on the CAGNICOURT Group of batteries, and in addition 22 other batteries were engaged. The Corps on our right assisted by engaging another 9 batteries.

Early this morning, after a heavy bombardment, the enemy attacked our position in the neighbourhood of POLDERHOEK Chateau. On the left the attack was repulsed, but on the right the enemy succeeded in occupying about 300 yards of our front line.

2. PRISONERS.

2 wounded prisoners, one of whom has since died, were captured this afternoon in U.21.a.

3. IDENTIFICATIONS.

(a) The body of a man of the 12th Coy., 3rd Battn., 14th B.I.R., 16th Bav. Div. was found at U.22.c 2.6. This man was killed during the attack on the afternoon of the 14th.

(b) Documents also establish the presence of the 1st Battn. of this regiment in the neighbourhood of BULLECOURT on the morning of the 14th.

4. MOVEMENT.

CENTRE SECTOR. Movement was seen about UNICORN and ULSTER Trenches, in the Sunken Road in U.15.c, and between there and HENDECOURT, round the CROW'S NEST, near OUSE LANE, and round MILL Ruins.

Men entered ULSTER Trench from HENDECOURT at U.4.c 6.1, also OPAL TRENCH at U.6.b 8.4.

At 1.45 p.m. 50 men and at 3.15 p.m. 40 men, in fatigue dress, left CROFT LANE at U.9.a 5.7 and went N.E.

OGRE PIT appears to be used as a dressing station.

LEFT SECTOR.

Usual movement was seen in BOW and OX Trenches.

5. WORK.

RIGHT SECTOR. Men were digging and carrying trench material near the Factory, also near the Sunken Road in U.15.c. and at U.22.b.5.3.

Much new chalk has been thrown up at U.22.b.1.7. and U.22.a.7.6.

Wire has been repaired in front of MORDEN TRENCH at U.17.c.3.1.

CENTRE SECTOR. Working parties were seen at the CROW'S NEST, and at U.15.a.4.3.

The enemy appears to be digging a trench between U.15.a.4.8-1.9.

LEFT SECTOR. Working parties were seen at the SCHMIDTHOHLE.

6. REPORTS OF PATROLS.

RIGHT SECTOR. The crater at C.6.d.5.7. was occupied, and at midnight much noise and shouting came from the Factory in U.22.

There was nothing else of importance to report.

CENTRE SECTOR. There was nothing unusual to report.

LEFT SECTOR. No hostile patrols were seen, and all was quiet.

7. GENERAL.

Movement of troops from RUSSIA to the West. According to reports and letters from Germany at the end of November, men who were then on leave from the front were being given 10 days extension on account of an intense railway movement, which was about to take place from Russia to the Western Front.

8. WEATHER FORECAST, noon 15th to noon 16th Dec.

Wind between W. and N.W. 15-20 mph., decreasing and probably changing towards N. Fair or fine at first, later cloudy with some showers probable. Good visibility. Temperature, day 40-45, night 30-35.

Wolyrles. Lieut.

for B.G.G.S.

SUNDAY, DECEMBER 16th.

Sun rises 7.50 a.m., sets 3.40 p.m.
Moon rises 9.29 a.m., sets 6.18 p.m.

40th Division. 1103/2/5. (G).

APP. IV

HEADQUARTERS No. 2/958/14 Date 21.12.17 229th FIELD COMPANY

H.Q., 40TH DIVISIONAL ENGINEERS. No. R 215/46 Date 21.12.17

Headquarters,

119th Infantry Brigade.

****

The following copy of remarks by the Corps Commander and Army Commander regarding the raid recently carried out by the 119th Infantry Brigade, is forwarded for information.

Copy to CRE

19th Decr. 1917.

Lieut-Colonel.
General Staff, 40th Division.

Third Army.
****

This small operation, carried out by the 40th Division is the complement of the attack made by the 3rd and 16th Divisions on the 20th November. The effect is that the Germans have been cleared out of the low ground a short distance W. of BULLECOURT and their dugouts and trenches have been destroyed therein with no inducements for them to return. The casualties we suffered are somewhat high, but the front was narrow, the enemy probably picked men with good cover and the operation had to be carried out by daylight.

I think that the operation was well planned and executed.

16th Decr. 1917.

(Sd) A. HALDANE, Lieut-General,
Commanding VI Corps.

VI Corps.
****

This appears to have been a most satisfactory and creditable operation, and the 40th Division are to be congratulated.

(Sd) J. B Y N G .

17.12.17.

General.

O.C. 229th by
To see & return

21/12/17

CRE 40th Div.

J App

CONFIDENTIAL.

40th DIVISION INTELLIGENCE SUMMARY No.27
8 a.m. 28th - 8 a.m. 29th December 1917.

I. OPERATIONS. (Our Own).

(a) INFANTRY. Patrols, accompanied by R.Es, went out and blew up ARGUS and VULCAN MEBUS. The map shows two posts in U.14.d, but it is believed that only one exists, viz. the one at U.14.d.-80.50 which is composed of a MEBU at its base with a trench 60 yards long and a dugout with M.G. emplacement above it at the front. This MEBU (now called ARGUS) has been destroyed and the dugout and M.G. emplacement will be destroyed to-night.
Another patrol established the fact that the small trench at U.21.b.25.90 was occupied and that M.G. fired from there.

Light T.Ms fired on the sunken road in U.14, the Aeroplane and FAG ALLEY, during the day.
M.T.Ms fired 29 rounds on Aeroplane, earthworks, and 25 rounds on KANDY TRENCH.

(b) Artillery. Movement in U.16.a and U.10.d was shelled and casualties inflicted (57 rounds).
50 rounds were used for cutting wire in front of trench at U.15.b.7.0.
140 rounds were fired on ULSTER TRENCH, UPTON QUARRY and U.21.b.5.7 to U.21.b.3.9.
390 rounds expended in night firing on various trenches and tracks.

II. HOSTILE ATTITUDE & ACTIVITY.

(a) Artillery. Generally quiet, except for shelling of NOW LANE at 10.45 p.m. with 30 rounds 15 cm.

(b) Movement. Much individual movement in COPSE TRENCH in U.15.a & b.
At 4 p.m. a party of 15 walking along COPSE ROAD in U.15.b towards FONTAINE was scattered by our artillery.
Two small parties fully equipped (20 and 15 men respectively) were seen on the HENDECOURT - CHERISY Road in U.3.b in the morning.
Several men seen during the day wearing caps with red bands.

(c) Aerial Activity. 7.30 a.m. 2 E.A. flew very low over our lines. 11 a.m. E.A. flew low over ST. LEGER and ERVILLERS. Between 1.30 and 2.30 p.m. E.A. patrolled our left sector.

III. HOSTILE DEFENCES.

(a) Work. New earth has been thrown up in ULSTER AVENUE and UNICORN TRENCH in U.10.a & b.

(b) Wire. New concertina wire has been put in front of the CROW'S NEST in U.11.b.

V. MISCELLANEOUS.

Battery of 4 77 mm. guns was seen firing from sunken road in O.36.b. H.A. informed and engaged it.

[signature] Captain,
General Staff, 40th Division.

29:12:17.

App VI

CONFIDENTIAL.

40th DIVISION INTELLIGENCE SUMMARY No.29.
Period 8 a.m. 30th - 8 a.m. 31st Dec.'17.

1. OPERATIONS (Our own).
(a) Infantry. RIGHT BRIGADE. NO MAN'S LAND was found to be clear of the enemy. Enemy posts reported yesterday in SELBY and RIPON appeared to be strongly held. Very lights were fired from PUDSEY SUPPORT.

CENTRE BRIGADE. Patrols thoroughly reconnoitred the front, without encountering the enemy. A machine gun fired from U.22.b.5.1. and the wire in front of this trench is 6 ft thick.

LEFT BRIGADE. Patrols went out and investigated ARGUS and the post at U.14.d.8.5. It is now established that ARGUS does not exist and the demolition of the post at U.14.d.8.5. was completed last night with R.E. assistance. Afterwards patrol proceeded E. of Sunken Road and found shell holes protected by concertina wire and several new rows of concertina and trip wire about 200 yards E. of the road. Enemy were working on new trench about U.15.c.3.8.

Another patrol found a thin belt of wire about U.21.b.2.8. and discovered the small trench at this point held by a party of the enemy with M.G.

Snipers fired at enemy as opportunity offered, but results could not be ascertained.

M.G's fired 2,000 rounds on OSTRICH AVENUE and BULLDOG SUPPORT and 5,000 rds in co-operation with artillery on U.22.b.6.7. and U.17.d.4.1.

Light T.M's fired on usual targets in Left Brigade area.
6" Newtons fired 17 rds into FAG ALLEY and 24 rds into KANDY TRENCH.

(b) Artillery
440 round concentration was fired between 5.10 and 5.20 p.m. on OSTRICH AVENUE - TERRIER ALLEY and sunken road U.18.c.35.10. to U.17.d.60.45.

50 rounds used for cutting wire in front of COPSE TRENCH and 1120 rds on shelling movement and miscellaneous targets throughout the day.

475 rds fired during the night on targets U A P 50, 51, 10, and U B P 6, 9 and 36, trenches, tracks and various important points.

II. HOSTILE ATTITUDE & ACTIVITY.
(a) Artillery. Hostile artillery was very active during the afternoon around TANK SUPPORT, LONDON SUPPORT and BULLECOURT. Several hundred rounds being fired. Otherwise shelling has been of a desultory character.

A few Gas shells were fired on back areas during the night.

(b) Movement.
7.30 a.m. man seen at sap C.6.b.3.3.
Movement observed at PUDSEY POST during the day.
Smoke was issuing from U.15.c.8.9. There was considerable movement between this point and U.15.a.8.3.

(c) N i l.

III. HOSTILE DEFENCES
(a) Work. Party at work on PUDSEY SUPPORT and digging observed in trench U.16.c.6.0.

There appears to be new trenches about U.23.a.50.75. and U.15.a.3.0.

(b) Wire. New wire put out at U.15.a.2.2. and wire considerably

thickened....

thickened at U.15.a.6.1.

(c) M.G's etc.
M.G's located at U.22.b.15.28 - U.22.d.95.80. - U.23.c.6.1. and suspected at U.15.c.3.3. Burst of M.G. fire during the night came from U.21.b.5.7.

V. MISCELLANEOUS.

There was unusual amount of rifle fire during the night opposite the Right Brigade and numerous Very Lights were put up by the enemy.

About 80 red rockets were sent up about U.9.d. at 7.5 a.m. No apparent action followed.

Captain,

General Staff, 40th D,vision.

31:12:17.

****

EXTRACTS FROM ARMY SUMMARY No.894.

OPERATIONS. THIRD ARMY. After heavy artillery fire the enemy attacked about 7.45 a.m. on a front of about 2500 yards from LA VACQUERIE northwards. A footing was gained in our trenches at the salient north-west of LA VACQUERIE and south of MARCOING. Subsequent counter-attacks are reported to have gained the salient north-west of LA VACQUERIE, but to have been unsuccessful on the left flank south of MARCOING.

GERMAN TROOPS WITH THE TURKISH ARMIES. (from G.H.Q. Summary).
(a) Ten German prisoners belonging to the 701st Inf. Bn. were captured by our troops in PALESTINE on the 27th December.
According to the statements of a prisoner captured earlier in December, the 701st, 702nd and 705th Inf. Bns. are all present in the area north of JERUSALEM.
(b) It is reported that, on the 9th Dec., a new formation about 3000 strong, composed of volunteers drawn from various units, was being assembled at depots in the BERLIN area, and was destined for service in PALESTINE.

NEW RED CROSS MARKS FOR STATIONARY HOSPITALS. French aerial photographs in the MEUSE area show a new type of Red Cross marking for German stationary hospital units, in the shape of a Black Cross on a white circular ground; the diameter of the circle varies from 17 to 25 yards, and the length of the arms of the cross from 12 to 14 yards. This mark is traced on the ground and is clearly visible in aerial photographs. Moreover, the white circle enables night-flying aeroplanes to recognise hospitals easily.

DRAFTING OF THE 1919 CLASS TO THE EASTERN THEATRE. On the 18th Dec., two trains containing men of the 1919 class are reported to have left DUTSBURG (VII Corps District) for Russia..
This corroborates previous reports that drafts of the 1919 Class are being sent from Germany to Russia to replace drafts of seasoned soldiers, who are being transferred to the Western Theatre.

Army Form C. 2118.

WAR DIARY
or
~~INTELLIGENCE SUMMARY.~~
(*Erase heading not required.*)

Instructions regarding War Diaries and Intelligence Summaries are contained in F. S. Regs., Part II. and the Staff Manual respectively. Title pages will be prepared in manuscript.

Hqrs 40th Divisional Engineers

Place	Date	Hour	Summary of Events and Information	Remarks and references to Appendices
GOMIECOURT	1/1/18		All Field Coys in the line – 2 Sections of 174 Tunnelling Coy RE attached for work.	HRR
	2/1/18		Routine – Hqrs 224 Fd Coy RE moved from back billets Ervillers to forward billets MOREUIL.	HRR
	3/1/18		Routine.	HRR
	4/1/18		CRE attended Conference at 6th Bde (119) Hqrs.	HRR
	5/1/18		Enemy attacked East of Bullecourt, but after obtaining a footing in our trenches in small numbers was successfully ejected. State 2 off 6 OR and 1 off 5 OR.	HRR
	6/1/18		Conference at Hqrs Divisional Engineers attended by Coy Commanders & OC 12th Yorks Regt (Pioneers).	HRR
BEHAGNIES	7/1/18		Hqrs 40th Divisional Engineers moved to BEHAGNIES. Lt Col G Goodwin (CRE) went to French School Chalons Sur Marne for 2 days, prior to proceeding on leave to U.K. Lt Col HW Becher DSO (12th Yorks Regt) Pioneers acting CRE in his place.	HRR

A5834 Wt. W4973/M687 750,000 8/16 D. D. & L. Ltd. Forms/C.2118/13.

Instructions regarding War Diaries and Intelligence Summaries are contained in F. S. Regs., Part II. and the Staff Manual respectively. Title pages will be prepared in manuscript.

Army Form C. 2118.

WAR DIARY
or
INTELLIGENCE SUMMARY.
(*Erase heading not required.*)

Hqrs 40th Divisional Engineers

Place	Date	Hour	Summary of Events and Information	Remarks and references to Appendices
BEHAGNIES	8/1/18		Tracing of new trench East of Bullecourt by 231 Fd Coy RE, digging of same (extension of FOXTROT from LONDON RESE to TANK SUPT about U28 b85) by 12th Yorks Regt (Pioneers) and wiring by infantry under supervision of 224 Fd Coy RE. 229 Fd Coy RE demolished MG emplacement & dugout in No Mans Land.	HRRA
	9/1/18		CE VI Corps visited these Hqrs	HRRA
	10/1/18		Routine -	HRRA
"	11/1/18	-	Orders issued for defences in Battle Zone, 15000 yds of trench to be wired & mostly dug to depth of 18 inches -	HRRA
"	12/1/18		State 1 off 6 OR Attd 2 off 6 OR -	HRRA
	16/1/18		Owing to collapse of trenches due to sudden thaw after frost, overland tracks are considered necessary & arrangements made to lay trench boards -	HRRA
	17/1/18		No 3 Section 181 Tunnelling Coy arrived at MORY for work under CRE 40th Div - Laying of trenchboard tracks continued	HRRA
"	18/1/18		" "	HRRA

A5834 Wt. W4973/M687 750,000 8/16 D. D. & L. Ltd. Forms/C.2118/13.

Army Form C. 2118.

WAR DIARY
or
INTELLIGENCE SUMMARY.
(*Erase heading not required.*)

Instructions regarding War Diaries and Intelligence Summaries are contained in F. S. Regs., Part II. and the Staff Manual respectively. Title pages will be prepared in manuscript.

Hqrs 40th Divisional Engineers —

Place	Date	Hour	Summary of Events and Information	Remarks and references to Appendices
JAN 1918				
BEHAGNIES	19/1/18		Routine – Digging & wiring of trenches in battle zone begun — State 1 off 5 OR att.d 2 off 7 OR –	HRRA
	20/1/18		Routine	
	21/1/18			HRRA
	22/1/18			
	23/1/18			
	24/1/18		CE VI Corps and CRE went round new defences in Battle Zone.	HRRA
	25/1/18		Scheme of tunnelled dug outs for Divisional, Bde and Group Hqrs submitted to 40th Div G	HRRA
	26/1/18		State 1 off 5 OR att.d 2 off 7 OR	HRRA
	27/1/18		Routine	HRRA
	28/1/18		Lt Col G Goodwin CRE returned from leave.	HRRA

A5834 Wt. W4973/M687 750,000 8/16 D. D. & L. Ltd. Forms/C.2118/13.

Instructions regarding War Diaries and Intelligence Summaries are contained in F. S. Regs., Part II. and the Staff Manual respectively. Title Pages will be prepared in manuscript.

WAR DIARY
or
~~INTELLIGENCE SUMMARY~~

(Erase heading not required.)

Army Form C. 2118

Hqrs 40th Divisional Engineers

Place	Date	Hour	Summary of Events and Information	Remarks and references to Appendices
BEHAGNIES	29/1/18		Routine – CRE (and 650 I) planned defence of NOREUIL	HRR A
	30/1/18		Routine – CRE (and 650 I) planned defence of ECOUST	
			467 and 469 Field Coys (59th Div) moved to ERVILLERS for work under CRE 40th Div –	HRR A
	31/1/18		467 and 469 Field Coys RE took over all work in back areas (camps, huts, stables etc) from Field Coys of 40th Div.	
			Reconnaissance by CRE of new track from IGAREE Corner (near NOREUIL) to front line – in extension of NOREUIL SWITCH (BATTLEZONE)	HRR A

H R Ruggles. Brice Capt RE
Adjt
40th Div Engineers 6/1/18

1875 Wt. W593/826 1,000,000 4/15 J.B.C. & A. A.D.S.S./Forms/C. 2118.

Instructions regarding War Diaries and Intelligence Summaries are contained in F. S. Regs., Part II. and the Staff Manual respectively. Title pages will be prepared in manuscript.

WAR DIARY
or
~~INTELLIGENCE SUMMARY.~~
(Erase heading not required.)

Army-Form C. 2118.

Hqrs 40th Divisional Engineers

Place	Date	Hour	Summary of Events and Information	Remarks and references to Appendices
BENAGNIES	1/2/18		Routine. 467th and 469th Field Coy. R.E. (59th Division) came under C.R.E. 40 Div. for work in back areas.	See C.R.E. order 199/4.
	2/2/18		Routine	HRR.H
	3/2/18		Conference of O.C's Field Coys at Div. Hqrs.	HRRA
	4/1/18		C.E. VI Corps and CRE went round Right Bde Sector	
	5/1/18			
	6/1/18		1 officer (229 Fd Coy R.E.) and 40 O.R. attd Infantry returned from Salvage area Saulty; average amount salved was 3 lorry loads daily, which included previously loading, conveying & off loading of stores from pontoon wagons near main road.	HRRA
	7/1/18		CRE 59th Division went round the line with CRE in view of oncoming relief	HRRA
	8/1/18		CRE went over new work on battle zone to be taken over from 34th Div on relief of 40th Div in the line	HRRA

A5834 Wt. W4973/M687 750,000 8/16 D. D. & L. Ltd. Forms/C.2118/13.

Instructions regarding War Diaries and Intelligence Summaries are contained in F. S. Regs., Part II. and the Staff Manual respectively. Title Pages will be prepared in manuscript.

WAR DIARY
or
~~INTELLIGENCE SUMMARY~~
(Erase heading not required.)

Army Form C. 2118

Hqrs 40th Divisional Engineers

Place	Date	Hour	Summary of Events and Information	Remarks and references to Appendices
BEHAGNIES	9/1/18		Routine	HWW
	10/1/18		467 Field Coy RE (59th Div) relieved 224 Fd Coy in 1st Sector - 224 Fd Coy moved to Hamelincourt - Reconnaissance made for demolishing bridges, Rlys. & roads in Div'area in event of hostile attack - C.R.E's Order No. 194/4 6/1/18.	HWW
	11/1/18		CE VI Corps & CRE went round the new trenches in the Battle Zone	HWW
	12/1/18		469 Field Coy RE (59th Div) relieved 231 Fd Coy in Centre Sector - 231 Fd Coy remained at MORY for work on digging & wiring in new Battle Zone	
			470 Fd Coy RE relieved 229 Fd Coy in left Sector - 229 Fd Coy moved to Henin, transport Mory CRE visited all Coy Hqrs -	HWW
GOMIECOURT	13/1/18		Hqrs 40th Div Engineers moved from BEHAGNIES to GOMIECOURT	
			CRE visited all Coy Hqrs. Work on Second System (Battle Zone) taken over from CRE 34th Div. Relief of 59th Div. by 40th Div. completed at 10-0am.	HWW CRE 34 Div. Ho. report 9/1/18
	14/1/18		CRE went round ECOUST CROISILLES Support Line in Battle zone & inspected 231 Fd Coy RE after lunch -	HWW
	15/1/18		CRE attended a demonstration of combined Infantry & Tank attack at BRAY-SUR-SOMME	HWW
	16.1.18		C.R.E and C.R.E. Corps. troops marked out 3rd line 2nd system of the Battle Zone. Post 24 to Shaft Trench. Capt. Ruggles. Brise M.C. R.E. Adjt. proceeded on 14 days leave to England. Capt. A Grantham RE taking over the duties of Adjutant.	A.G.

875 Wt. W593/826 1,000,000 4/15 J.B.C. & A. A.D.S.S./Forms/C. 2118.

Instructions regarding War Diaries and Intelligence Summaries are contained in F. S. Regs., Part II. and the Staff Manual respectively. Title pages will be prepared in manuscript.

WAR DIARY
or
INTELLIGENCE SUMMARY.
(Erase heading not required.)

Army Form C. 2118.

Place	Date	Hour	Summary of Events and Information	Remarks and references to Appendices
Gomiecourt	17-2-18		229th Field Coy + 231st Field Coy each with parties of infantry 600 strong started work on Battle lines	R.G. ~~C.R.E. instruction dated 11-2-18~~
	18-2-18		C.R.E. inspected 224th Field Coy. R.E. at Hamelincourt. C.E. visited Divl Hqs.	R.G.
	19-2-18		C.R.E. went with C.E. to the left sector of the Corps to mark out a new 2nd system line	R.G.
	20-2-18		Routine.	R.G.
	21-2-18		229th Field Coy were inspected by C.R.E. at Henin.	R.G.
	22-2-18		Routine	R.G.
	23-2-18		C.R.E. attended conference at Div. Hqs.	R.G.
	24-2-18		Routine.	R.G.
	25-2-18		"	R.G.
	26-2-18		Warning order received that Division would probably move on the 28th to the Basseux Area. C.E. VI Corps visited Divnl R.E. Hqs. Order issued that 224 Field Coy. would come under C.E. VI Corps for work taking down 2 Casualty Clearing Stations near Boisleux St. Marc and re-erecting same at Le Bac de Sud on the Arras Doullens Road. 229th and 231st Field Coys. finished working on the Battle Line	41st Div. O. 127 R.G. 26.2.18
	27-2-18		224th Field Coy started work taking down No. 43 Casualty Clearing Station. 2 sections being accommodated and rationed by No. 43 C.C.S.	R.G.

A5834 Wt. W4973/M687 750,000 8/16 D. D. & L. Ltd. Forms/C.2118/13.

Instructions regarding War Diaries and Intelligence Summaries are contained in F. S. Regs., Part II. and the Staff Manual respectively. Title pages will be prepared in manuscript.

WAR DIARY
or
INTELLIGENCE SUMMARY.
(Erase heading not required.)

Army Form C. 2118.

Place	Date	Hour	Summary of Events and Information	Remarks and references to Appendices
Basseux	28.2.18		Divisional Hqs. moved from Gomiecourt to Basseux. Hqs. 224th Field Coy. and 2 sections moved from Hamelincourt to Bailleulmont, 229th Field Coy moved from Henin to Barly, and 231 Field Coy from Mory to Bienvillers. The 40th Division (less Artillery) came into G.H.Q. Reserve at 12 noon, prepared to move at 24 hours notice.	A.G. 40th Div. [illegible] No. 120 of 26/2/18

[illegible signature] Capt. R.E.
a/Adjt.
40th Divl. R.E.

A5834 Wt. W4973/M687 750,000 8/16 D. D. & L. Ltd. Forms/C.2118/13.

H.

O.C. 224th. Field Co. RE.
O.C. 229th. Field Co. RE.
O.C. 231st. Field Co. RE.
O.C. 467th. Field Co. RE.
O.C. 469th. Field Co. RE.
40th. Division (Q) for information.

---

1. 467 and 469th Field Companies, RE. come under C.R.E. 40th. Division for work in back areas from to-morrow, 31st. instant, inclusive.

2. They move today into DYSART and South ERVILLERS Camps.

3. All work as per attached list will be handed over by 224th. 229th and 231st. Field Companies, RE. respectively where concerned.

4. Location of Field Companies, R.E. of 40th. Division:-

224th. Field Co. RE. (Rear)	ERVILLERS,	B.20.a.2.2.
229th. Field Co. RE.	ST. LEGER.	T.28.c.9.1.
231st. Field Co. RE.	(Tunnellers Camp MORY).	B.22.b.7.7.

War Diary -

H.R. Rugg[?] Capt RE

30-1-18. for C.R.E. 40th. Division.

Traverses around Ammn dump Boyelles Rd.
Vaux Road.
RE Bde HQ
RFA " HQ
469 Ambulance Hut (Sucrerie) 231
Dysart Camp.
[illegible] Stables

SECRET

Copy No. 6....

40th DIVISION WARNING ORDER NO.127.
****

26/2/18.

Ref. map
LENS 11. 1:100,000.

War Diary

1. The 34th Division will take over the Centre Sector of the VI Corps front between 1st and 3rd March.

2. The 34th Div. Artillery will relieve the 40th Divisional Artillery in the Centre Sector of the VI Corps front on the nights of 3rd/4th and 4th/5th March.

3. The two Machine Gun Companies 40th Division now at the disposal of 3rd and 59th Divisions will rejoin the 40th Division on the 3rd March.

The 40th Division M.G.Battalion less 2 companies now in VI Corps Reserve will remain at ENNISKILLEN and DURHAM 'B' CAMP, MERCATEL until 3rd March when they will rejoin 40th Division.

4. The following is a forecast of the moves necessitated by the above relief :-

Feb. 28th. 40th Division less Artillery and M.G.BN. from BOISLEUX (late GOMIECOURT) Area to BASSEUX Staging Area relieving 34th Division.
40th Divl. H.Qrs to BASSEUX.

March 2nd. 34th Divl. Artillery from SOUASTRE Area to Wagon Lines 40th Division.

March 3rd. A Brigade 40th Division from GOUY Bde Group Area to BLAIRVILLE Brigade Group Area.

40th Div. Machine Gun Battalion to BLAIREVILLE Area.

March 5th. 40th Divisional Artillery to SOUASTRE Area.

5. ACKNOWLEDGE. J.G.

[signature]
Captain,
General Staff, 40th Division.

Issued at 10.30 am.......

****

Copy No. 1 to G.O.C.
2 119th I.B.
3 120th I.B.
4 121st I.Bde.
5 C.R.A.
6 C.R.E.
7 12th York. R.
8 D.M.G.Bn:
9 Signals
10 A.D.M.S.
11. to D.A.D.V.S.
12 A.P.M.
13 D.A.D.O.S.
14 D.Gas Off.
15 Div Train
16 Supply Col.
17 Camp Comdt.
18 "Q"
19 VI Corps
20 VI Corps Arty.
21 to 3rd Div.
22 59th Div.
23 34th Div.
24 & 25 War Diary
26 File

S E C R E T.

H.Q.,
40TH DIVISIONAL
ENGINEERS.
No. 194/U
Date 6.2.18

O.C. 224th. Field Co. RE.
O.C. 229th. Field Co. RE.
O.C. 231st. Field Co. RE.
O.C. 467th. Field Co. RE. (for information)
O.C. 469th. Field Co. RE. " "
O.C. 470th. Field Co. RE. " "
40th. Division "G". " "
40th. Division "Q" " "
C.R.E. 59th. Division. " "

---

1. The following movements will take place on:-

	10th. Feb.	11th. Feb.	12th. Feb.
224th Field Co.	Right sector to ERVILLERS. (Camp of 467th Field Co. RE.)	ERVILLERS to HAMELINCOURT. (207th F.Co. billets)	
467th.Field Co.	ERVILLERS to Right Sector.		
231st. Field Co.		Centre Sector to MORY.	No change in H.Qtrs Camp of 231st F. Coy
469th. Field Co.		MORY to Centre Sector.	
229th. Field Co.			Left Sector to HENIN and H.Qtrs, MORY. (208th F.C. billets)
470th. Field Co.			ERVILLERS to Left Sector.

If desired the 224th. Field Co. RE. can move direct to HAMELINCOURT on the 10th. instant.

2. The 207th. 208th and 209th. Field Companies, RE. vacate their present Camps on the 9th instant, and the opposite numbers of the 40th. Division Field Companies must have advance parties to take over the billets early on that day.

3. The Field Companies, R.E. of the 34th. Division are situated as follows:-

207th. Field Co. R.E.	HAMELINCOURT.
208th. Field Co. R.E.	H.Qtrs. & Transport Lines, MORY. B.20.a.4.6. O.C. & 4 Sections at HENIN.N.32.a. (left hand side of road, HENIN to NEUVILLE VITASSE).
209th. Field Co. R.E.	MORY. B.21.d.5.8.

4. The Works Companies will rejoin their Units on arrival in the Reserve area.

G. J. Godwin

Lieut.Colonel, RE

6.2.18.

C.R.E., 40th. Division.

SECRET

O.C. 224th. Field Co. R.E.
O.C. 229th. Field Co. R.E.
O.C. 231st. Field Co. R.E.
O.C. 467th. Field Co. R.E. (for information)
O.C. 469th. Field Co. R.E. " "
O.C. 470th. Field Co. R.E. " "
40th. Division "G" " "
40th. Division "Q" " "
C.R.E. 59th. Division. " "
C.R.E. 34th. Division. " "

H.Q.
40TH DIVISIONAL
ENGINEERS.
No. 194/4
Date 6.2.18

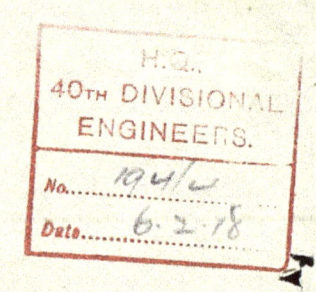

Reference this Office No. 194/4, of 6th inst., para 3:
for "H.Qtrs. & Transport Lines, MORY. B.20.a.4.6.
read "H.Qtrs. & Transport Lines, MORY. B.28.a.4.6."

H.R. Rowlandson

Captain, R.E.

6.2.18. for C.R.E., 40th. Division.

SECRET.

Copy No. 6....

26/2/18.

40th DIVISION ORDER NO. 128.

Ref. map LENS 11.
1:100,000.

1. Reference 40th Div. Warning Order No. 127 dated 2?/2/18, moves will take place in accordance with attached table. *

2. The 40th Division (less Artillery) will come into G.H.Q. Reserve at 12 noon on 28th February and will be prepared to move at 24 hours notice.

3. The 40th Divisional Artillery will come into G.H.Q. Reserve at 6.0 a.m. March 5th and will be prepared to move at 24 hours notice.

4. The 40th Div. M.G.Bn: less 3 Coys will move from ENNISKILLEN to ARMAGH Camp on the morning of 28th February. They will be in VI Corps Reserve and will receive orders direct from those headquarters.

5. "Q" will arrange for movement of any Details not mentioned in this order. They will also arrange for any additional transport required.

6. All hutments, camps and horselines will be handed over in a perfectly clean condition and certificates of cleanliness obtained.

7. Completion of moves will be reported to Div. H.Qrs. Reported AG.

8. Divisional Headquarters will close at GOMIECOURT at 12 noon 28th February and will re-open at BASSEUX at that hour.

9. ACKNOWLEDGE. AG.

W Carter
Captain,
General Staff, 40th Division.

Issued at......

Copy No. 1 to	G.O.C.	11 to	D.A.D.V.S.	21 to	3rd Div.
2	119th I.B.	12	A.P.M.	22	59th Div.
3	120th I.B.	13	D.A.D.O.S.	23	34th Div.
4	121st I.B.	14	D.G.O	24 & 25.	War Diary
5	C.R.A.	15	Train	26	File
6	C.R.E.	16	Supply Col.		
7	12th York.	17	C.Condt.		
8	D.M.G.Bn.	18	"Q"		
9	Signals	19	VI Corps		
10	A.D.M.S.	20	VI Corps Arty.		

* Table follows

40th Divisional Engineers.

WAR DIARY

C. R. E.

40th DIVISION

MARCH 1 9 1 8

Instructions regarding War Diaries and Intelligence Summaries are contained in F. S. Regs., Part II. and the Staff Manual respectively. Title pages will be prepared in manuscript.

WAR DIARY

~~or~~

~~INTELLIGENCE SUMMARY.~~

(Erase heading not required.)

Headquarters 40th DIVNL. ENGINEERS.

Army Form C. 2118.

Place	Date	Hour	Summary of Events and Information	Remarks and references to Appendices
BASSEUX.	1.3.18	-	C.R.E. visited all Coys.	R.G.
"	2.3.18	-	Letter received from 40 Divn. with copy of letter from VI Corps expressing the appreciation of the Corps Commander, of the work done by Field Coys on the Battle line.	40 Divn. APP I 112/22 G 4/3/18 R.G.
"	3.3.18	-	State 2 off 7 OR. att: 1 off 7 OR. All leave stopped from and including boat sailing March 5. 229th Field Coy. R.E. moved from Barly, (Gouy Area) with 119 Brigade Group, to billets at Hendecourt - in the Blairville Area.	R.G. 3/3/18
"	4.3.18	-	C.R.E. inspected 231 Field Coy R.E. at BIENVILLERS.	
"	5/3/18		Routine - CRE visited VI Corps Hqrs -	HRRB
"	6/3/18		CRE attended Conference at DHQ -	HRRB
"	7/3/18		Routine -	HRRB
"	8/3/18		The Corps Commander inspected the 40th Division by Brigade Groups - The Field Coys paraded with their respective brigades -	HRRB
"	9/3/18		CRE went round the defences on the Corps Left front Wancourt to Henin area - State:- 2 off: 7 OR att'd 1 off. 10 OR -	HRRB
"	10/3/18		Routine: CRE's orders for Field Companies while the division is in GHQ Reserve - see App III	HRRB APP III

A5834 Wt. W4973/M687 750,000 8/16 D. D. & L. Ltd. Forms/C.2118/13.

Army Form C. 2118.

WAR DIARY
or
~~INTELLIGENCE~~ SUMMARY.
(Erase heading not required.)

Instructions regarding War Diaries and Intelligence Summaries are contained in F. S. Regs., Part II. and the Staff Manual respectively. Title pages will be prepared in manuscript.

Headquarters 40th Divisional Engineers

Place	Date	Hour	Summary of Events and Information	Remarks and references to Appendices
BASSEUX	11/3/18		Routine. 224 Fd Coy RE stopped work on the new CCS (A5 2) Bac de Sud. Coys at rest.	HRRS
	12/3/18		Field Coys marched with Brigade Groups to new areas, 224 Fd Coy RE to Hendecourt (No 6 Camp) 229 Fd Coy RE to Durham B Camp Boisleux St Marc, 231 Fd Coy RE to Armagh Camp near Hamelincourt, so as to be in close move in the event of an enemy offensive on this front.	HRRS
	13/3/18		Companies resting & training.	HRRS
	14/3/18		ditto.	HRRS
	15/3/18		"	
	16/3/18		224 & 229 Fd Coys RE repairing Rifle Ranges. State 2 off 5 OR. Att: 1 off. 14 OR	HRRS
	17/3/18		229 Fd Coy repairing range. 231 Fd Coy provided working party of 100 OR to dig trench for buried cable in neighbourhood of HENIN under VI Corps Signal Officer. 224 Fd Coy RE completed repair of range near Hendecourt.	HRRS
	18/3/18		229 Fd Coy RE continued work on Rifle Range & 231 Fd Coy provided similar working party at HENIN. Deserter stated that enemy offensive was dated to start today, but it did not take place. 224 Fd Coy RE started technical training	HRRS

WAR DIARY
or
~~INTELLIGENCE SUMMARY.~~
(Erase heading not required.)

Instructions regarding War Diaries and Intelligence Summaries are contained in F. S. Regs., Part II. and the Staff Manual respectively. Title pages will be prepared in manuscript.

Army Form C. 2118.

Hqrs 40th Divisional Engineers –

Place	Date	Hour	Summary of Events and Information	Remarks and references to Appendices
BASSEUX	19/3/18		224 Fd Coy RE continue technical training 229 Fd Coy RE Started work on the erection of a breastwork for Anti-aircraft defence round a YMCA hut Boisleux au Mont. 231 Fd Coy RE Continued work on new cable trench near Ablain –	HRRS
	20/3/18		CRE went to MERCATEL & NEUVILLE VITASSE to see OC 229 Fd Coy regarding alterations to a rifle range & repairs to a road for HA. Orders received to go into the line in relief of 3rd Division on the 22nd & 23rd. Coys at work as above – CRE visited 3rd DHQ (BOISLEUX AU MONT) with view to taking over from them in the line – (App IV)	HRRS
HAMELINCOURT	21/3/18		Enemy ~~commenced~~ offensive on Corps front started 5.0 am. 224 & 229 Fd Coys RE moved to ARMAGH camp HAMELINCOURT joining 231st Fd Coy already there & 12th Yorks Regt Pioneers to ECOUMEZ camp HAMELINCOURT. Enemy penetrated our lines taking Bullecourt ECOUST NOREUIL & LAGNICOURT – Field Coys & Pioneers ordered to hold ARMY LINE in front of Hamelincourt under CRE. Hqrs Div RE moved to HAMELINCOURT – Fd Coys & Pioneers remained continuously in these trenches until the morning of the 23rd.	HRRS
	22/3/18		Enemy attack continued, mostly threatening ST LEGER but stout resistance was successfully offered by troops of this division on the Southern side. DHQ less Hqrs RE moved to BUCQUOY – R.E. HQ. Office at BUCQUOY All first line transport less limbers & watercarts moved back to DOUCHY LES-AYETTE	HRRS

A5834 Wt. W4973/M687 750,000 8/16 D. D. & L. Ltd. Forms/C.2118/13.

Instructions regarding War Diaries and Intelligence Summaries are contained in F. S. Regs., Part II. and the Staff Manual respectively. Title pages will be prepared in manuscript.

WAR DIARY
or
INTELLIGENCE SUMMARY.
(Erase heading not required.)

Army Form C. 2118.

Place	Date	Hour	Summary of Events and Information	Remarks and references to Appendices
GOMIECOURT	23/3/18		Hd Qrs R.E. moved early morning to GOMIECOURT – 3 Fd Coys and 12th Yorks R. (P) ordered to man trenches west of and parallel to BEHAGNIES – ERVILLERS road – all moved in during morning & began to consolidate the position – transport to GOMIECOURT. GOC met CRE at 121st I.B. HdQrs in GOMIECOURT 2.30 pm and gave orders for the consolidation of the 5th system – EAST of GOMIECOURT to WEST of SAPIGNIES. CRE traced out 10 posts from B25c to H1c and 229 + 231 Fd C. & 1½ coys Pioneers were withdrawn from the line & dug these posts to a depth of 3 ft. Four lorry loads of wire were brought up during the night & dumped at 3 points behind this line. State 2 off 7 OR wd 12 OR –	H.R.N.
"	24/3/18		Work by 2 coys & Pioneers continued as above during night – ½ Pioneer Bn & 224 Fd Coy still holding the support line W of main road. CRE met CRE 41st Div at H, C83 9.30 am and agreed on the point of crossing of new defensive line with IV Corps Boundary. CRE sent OC 229 Fd Coy to meet CRE 31st Div at 11 am at A23 a b c for similar arrangement and to trace a chain of posts from this point Southwards East of GOMIECOURT. CRE met CRE Corps troops at DHQ BUCQUOY at 11 am to report progress for CE's information. He learnt here that the 42nd Division was to relieve 40th Div the following day & proceeded to 42nd Div HQ at ADINFER to make arrangements but was unable to find him. In reply to a wire CRE 42nd Div arrived at GOMIECOURT in evening and all particulars were given to him. Heavy fighting continued during the night and at about 10 pm 231 Fd Coy & the Pioneers working on the rear line were withdrawn to hold the trenches East of GOMIECOURT and 229 Fd C. lined the hollow road in A23a. The situation appeared less grave at about 1 am & these units then resumed work until dawn. The Relief ordered by 40th Div order No 136 of 24/3/18 att was deferred – Guides were sent as ordered under § 4 (d) – but did not meet those from 42nd Div.	H.R.N.
"	25/3/18		Enemy advance continued during the day – the support line partly held by Pioneers & 224 Fd Coy now became front line and these units took a prominent part in repelling enemy attacks. CRE notified about 3 pm that the sector had passed at 10.30 am to GOC 42nd Div. CRE issued orders for the relief of Pioneers & Field Coys after arrangement with G.O.C. 125th Inf: Bde. 229 + 231 Fd Coys handed over work to 427 + 429 Fd C.	H.R.N.

Instructions regarding War Diaries and Intelligence Summaries are contained in F. S. Regs., Part II. and the Staff Manual respectively. Title pages will be prepared in manuscript.

WAR DIARY
or
INTELLIGENCE SUMMARY.
(Erase heading not required.)

Army Form C. 2118.

Place	Date	Hour	Summary of Events and Information	Remarks and references to Appendices
GOMIECOURT	25/3/18 continued		and marched for DOUCHY-LES-AYETTE. 224 F.C. & Pioneers relieved in the line during the night and followed them. GOMIECOURT was heavily shelled during the day. Divl HQ RE left about 6.30 pm on foot and reached D.HQ at MONCHY-AU-BOIS via COURCELLES and AYETTE at 6.45 am.	Losses since 21/3/18: 229 F.C. 6 OR wounded; 224 " nil; 231 " 1 killed, 2 wounded. Pioneers: 3 offrs wounded, 3 OR killed, 19 " wounded, 40 " missing, 3 " wounded at duty
BAILLEULMONT and HABARQ	26/3/18		In consequence of a report that the enemy had penetrated the line at HEBUTERNE and was threatening our right flank 229, 231 F.Coys & Pioneers were ordered to place BIENVILLERS in a state of defence and to prepare all approaches from the South for obstruction. Defences were placed under direction of Maj. CLARK RE. 224 F.C. ordered to take similar steps at MONCHY-AU-BOIS.	
			D.HQ moved to BAILLEULMONT in morning. C.R.E. went via BERLES-AU-BOIS & BIENVILLERS and saw all Coys en route. D.HQ to HABARCQ in evening. Field Coys & Pioneers were ordered to HABARCQ.	HRRB
WARLUZEL	27.3.18		Field Coys directed in morning to SOMBRIN and Pioneers to BEAUDRICOURT. H.Qrs Divl RE moved to WARLUZEL. Remainder of D.HQ to LUCHEUX. C.R.E. saw all Field Coys and Pioneers on the march.	HRRB
LUCHEUX	28.3.18		Orders issued to Field Coys at night to collect bridging equipment at LAHERLIERE. ~~orders~~ Coys & Pioneers rested during the day	HRRB
CHELERS	29.3.18		Orders to Field Coys & Pioneers to march to MONCHY-BRETON area in Brigade groups. They marched as follows from SOMBRIN - 224 F.C. to ORLENCOURT - 229 to LA COMTÉ. 231 to ROCOURT. Pioneers to TINQUES and TINQUETTE. D.H.Q. with C.R.E. to CHELERS	HRRB
	30.3.18		224 & 231 Fd Coys RE moved by lorry with Bde groups, Transport by road, to Doulieu & Sailly-sur-la-Lys areas. Lt Col H C Bayley DSO RE returned from England & resumed the duties of C.R.E. State 20 off 70 OR. Att. 1 off 14 OR. Lt Col G J P Goodwin RE left to take up appointment of CRE 66 Div.	HRRB
	31.3.18		231 Fd Coy RE relieved 502 Fd Coy RE (57th Div) in the line. 505 Fd Coy RE with view to taking over left Sector on 1st April - 224 Fd Coy RE relieved. Hqrs RE moved to MERVILLE & came under XV Corps.	HRRB

H R Ruggles-Brise Capt RE
for CRE 40th Div 1/4/18

A5834 Wt. W4973/M687 750,000 8/16 D. D. & L. Ltd. Forms/C.2118/13.

VI Corps No. GX. 599/146.

40th Division.

H.Q., 40TH DIVISIONAL ENGINEERS.
No. W 1/25
Date 3. 3. 18

****

The Corps Commander desires me to express to you his appreciation of the good work carried out by the Field Companies and Working parties of the 40th Division in the Battle Zone.

(Sd) R.H.KEARSLEY,

VI Corps.
1stMarch,1918.

B. G. G. S.

- ii -

40th Div. No. 1112/22(G).

C.R.E. 119th Inf. Bde.
120th ,,
121st ,,

*****

The Divisional Commander directs me to inform you of his appreciation of the excellent work done by the R.E. and Infantry, and wishes the above letter circulated to all concerned.

~~Lieut.~~ Col.
General Staff, 40th Division.

2/3/18.

**

40th Divisional Engineers.

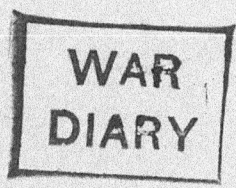

WAR DIARY

C. R. E.

40th DIVISION.

APRIL 1 9 1 8

Appendices attached:-

Destruction of Bridges.
Narratime of Operations 8th-12th April

Vol 22

Vol 23

Confidential

WAR DIARY

H Q^rs R.E. 40th DIVISION

April 1918

Instructions regarding War Diaries and Intelligence Summaries are contained in F. S. Regs., Part II. and the Staff Manual respectively. Title pages will be prepared in manuscript.

Army Form C. 2118.

WAR DIARY
or
~~INTELLIGENCE~~ SUMMARY.

(Erase heading not required.)

Hqrs 40th Divisional Engineers

Place	Date	Hour	Summary of Events and Information	Remarks and references to Appendices
MERVILLE	1/4/18		224 Fd Coy RE took over the work in left sector from 505 Fd Coy RE (57 Div) – SPADE RE dumps + workshops taken over – In addition to ordinary personnel, 15 men civilians, French + 54 women employed, the latter making camouflage for Corps.	[illegible]
CROIX du BAC	2/4/18		Divisional Hqrs (Ex Hqrs RA) moved to CROIX du BAC – 229 Fd Coy RE took over work from 421 Fd Coy RE (57 Div) 12th Yorks Regt (Pioneers) moved from Rue du Bois to Bac St Maur – CRE held conference of Coy Commanders at 229 Fd Coy RE's Hqrs – Corps Camouflage officer attended with regard to camouflaging of Emergency Bridges across the LYS –	[illegible]
	3/4/18		CE XV Corps visited these Hqrs – Conference of Coy Commanders at DHQ –	[illegible]
	4/4/18		Congratulatory messages from the King, the Army Commander (1st Army) and Corps Commander XI Corps on defence put up by the division during the recent fighting published in Divisional Routine Orders. Working party of 50 men supplied daily by Brigade in Reserve to each Fd Coy for work in Battle Zone. Routine.	[illegible]
	5/4/18		Personnel (apart from civilians) employed at SPADE dumps & workshops RE 17 OR. 12th Yorks Pioneers 30 OR. Party of 8 OR 12th Yorks P sent to Corps dump LA GORGUE as loading party.	[illegible]

A5834 Wt. W4973/M687 750,000 8/16 D. D. & L. Ltd. Forms/C.2118/13.

Army Form C. 2118.

WAR DIARY
or
INTELLIGENCE SUMMARY.
(Erase heading not required.)

Instructions regarding War Diaries and Intelligence Summaries are contained in F. S. Regs., Part II. and the Staff Manual respectively. Title pages will be prepared in manuscript.

Hqrs 40th Divisional Engineers –

Place	Date	Hour	Summary of Events and Information	Remarks and references to Appendices
CROIX du BAC	6/4/18		Routine – CRE went round MG positions with OC Div MG Battn – Stats 30ff. 8 OR. Att'd 1off. 10 OR –	ARees
	7/4/18		Routine – CE XV Corps visited these Hqrs – Emergency cork bridges over R. Lys completed –	ARees
	8/4/18		Arrangements made for 75 to 100 Infantry from each Bde to be attached to Fd Coys as Works Coys – Reconnaissance by CRE of Right Bde sector for new belt of wire –	ARees
VIEUX BERQUIN	9/4/18		Enemy offensive started on XV Corps front, forcing back the Portuguese division on our right, and exposing our right flank – In the morning Field Coys swung the cork and pontoon bridges across the R. LYS to facilitate retirement or Counter attack – The bridgeheads were heavily shelled all day – The enemy advance however continued and it became necessary to demolish the bridges – ~~Of~~ 23 permanent pontoon and emergency cork bridges ~~3~~ were successfully destroyed, many of them under enemy Machine Gun or Rifle fire. All Field Coy Transport was ordered back to West of DOULIEU. Hqrs RE moved to VIEUX BERQUIN – Field Coys continued to defend the North bank of the River Lys – The enemy succeeded in crossing the River later. The Permanent bridge at Sailly was only partially destroyed & the demolition of the permanent bridge at Estaires completely failed owing to primers failing to detonate – See Appendix I. The lesson to be learnt is that the utmost care should be taken to construct magazines as dry as possible as these primers evidently failed from the magazines not being dry enough.	ARees APP I

A5834 Wt. W4973/M687 750,000 8/16 D. D. & L. Ltd. Forms/C.2118/13.

Instructions regarding War Diaries and Intelligence Summaries are contained in F. S. Regs., Part II. and the Staff Manual respectively. Title pages will be prepared in manuscript.

WAR DIARY
or
~~INTELLIGENCE SUMMARY.~~
(Erase heading not required.)

Army Form C. 2118.

Hqrs 40th Divisional Engineers –

Place	Date	Hour	Summary of Events and Information	Remarks and references to Appendices
VIEUX BERQUIN	10/4/18		Field Companies concentrated at their Transport Lines West of DOULIEU and were ordered to support the 119 Inf Bde and later to defend LA VERRIER (~~under~~ ~~GOC 119 Inf Bde~~) – They held the front line, order from left to right 229, 224, 231 Field Coy, with 88th Bde 29th Div on left flank and a battalion of Loyal N. Lancs operating with 120 Bde on Right flank – Coy Transport proceeded to MERRIS and later to West of STRAZEELE. 145 AT Coy RE who had been working under CRE XV Corps Troops came under command of CRE, remaining in the line with the Infantry.	NRAN
AU SOUVERAIN	11/4/18		Field Companies remained in the line throughout the day, in the evening forming a defensive flank in view of a counterattack by the 31st Division – Field Coys were relieved at night by a battalion of the Durham Light Infantry and proceeded to rejoin their transport lines W of STRAZEELE. Hqrs RE moved to Au Souverain –	NRAN
	12/4/18		Coy Transport moved to HONDEGHEM – Field Coys were ordered to dig a chain of posts in front of STRAZEELE in conjunction with the Infantry, the Enemy having attacked along the whole front and reported to have	NRAN

A5834 Wt. W4973/M687 750,000 8/16 D. D. & L. Ltd. Forms/C.2118/13.

Instructions regarding War Diaries and Intelligence Summaries are contained in F. S. Regs., Part II. and the Staff Manual respectively. Title pages will be prepared in manuscript.

WAR DIARY
or
~~INTELLIGENCE SUMMARY.~~
(Erase heading not required.)

Army Form C. 2118.

Hqrs 40th Divisional Engineers.

Place	Date	Hour	Summary of Events and Information	Remarks and references to Appendices
	13/4/18 Contd		broken through at NEUF BERQUIN – Picks and shovels were sent up for this purpose – 145 A T Coy RE ordered to report to CRE XV Corps troops at Wardrecques, proceeding there on 13th –	HAMS
RENESCURE	13/4/18		Work continued on digging of new chain of posts – In the evening Coys ordered to withdraw to their transport lines and to proceed to West of STAPLES, the division being withdrawn from the battle – Hqrs RE moved to RENESCURE. Narrative of operations 8/9th to 11/12th App II attached – Stats 3 off 9 OR – att 1 off 14 OR –	HAMS APP II
LONGUENESSE	14/4/18		Field Coys moved to CORMETTE – Hqrs RE to LONGUENESSE –	HAMS
	15/4/18		Coys resting –	HAMS

A5834 Wt. W4973/M687 750,000 8/16 D. D. & L. Ltd. Forms/C.2118/13.

Instructions regarding War Diaries and Intelligence Summaries are contained in F. S. Regs., Part II. and the Staff Manual respectively. Title pages will be prepared in manuscript.

WAR DIARY
or
~~INTELLIGENCE SUMMARY.~~
(Erase heading not required.)

Army Form C. 2118.

Hqrs 40th Divisional Engineers

Place	Date	Hour	Summary of Events and Information	Remarks and references to Appendices
WIZERNES	16/4/18		CRE inspected all Coys on parade – Hqrs RE moved to WIZERNES	HAMS
			Casualties during operations from 9th inst to 16th: 224 Fd Coy RE – Killed 1 Off 2 OR, Wounded 31 OR, Missing 7 OR; 229 – Killed 3 OR, Wounded 1 Off 27 OR, Missing 9 OR; 231 – Killed 1 Off 3 OR, Wounded 24 OR, Missing 12 OR	
	17/4/18		Coys training & at rest	HAMS
	18/4/18		GOC inspected all Field Coys on parade – Division transferred from XV to VIIIth Corps. Composite Brigade formed to which 224 Fd Coy attached under GOC 121 Bde –	HAMS
	19/4/18		CRE inspected 40th Div Signal Coy on parade – Appreciation of services of the division from Army, Corps & Divisional Commanders received.	HAMS
	20/4/18		Coys resting and training – State 2 Off 7 OR – att'd 1 Off 8 OR.	HAMS
	21/4/18		224 Fd Coy RE moved with Composite Brigade to STAPLE area & on to S of Oudezeele 229 moved to DIFQUES 231 " " ZUTOVE	HAMS

A5834 Wt. W4973/M687 750,000 8/16 D. D. & L. Ltd. Forms/C.2118/13.

Instructions regarding War Diaries and Intelligence Summaries are contained in F. S. Regs., Part II. and the Staff Manual respectively. Title pages will be prepared in manuscript.

WAR DIARY
or
INTELLIGENCE SUMMARY.
(Erase heading not required.)

Army Form C. 2118.

Hqrs 40th Divisional Engineers

Place	Date	Hour	Summary of Events and Information	Remarks and references to Appendices
WIZERNES	22/4/18		CRE proceeded to XV Corps Hqrs to see the Corps Commander with regard to laying out of new line in front of CASSEL – (Hezeele – Le Brearde line)	HAWS
			231 Fd Coy RE moved to East of St Sylvestre Cappel, personnel by bus, transport by road	
	23/4/18		CRE accompanied the Corps Commander round the new system of trenches between Hezeele and Le Brearde –	HAWS
			Personnel of the division (less Composite Brigade RA RE MG Bn for present) ordered to the Base, Cadres of formations alone remaining –	
			Hqrs RE moved to RWELD (DHQ remaining at WIZERNES)	
RWELD	24/4/18		229 Fd Coy RE moved, personnel by bus, transport by road, to SE of St Marie-Cappel. All Coys employed on digging new line – Composite brigade (121 Inf Bde) supplied daily working parties to 224 Fd Coy, every available man being employed on this work – 212 Fd Coy 33rd Div worked on Rgt Sector with 229 & 231 Fd Coys, but later rejoined its division –	HAWS
	25/4/18		Work continued as above. CRE being responsible for Rgt and Centre Sectors about 13000 yds of line. Posts of 20' with gaps of 30' being dug, concealed behind hedge rows. The Right Sector was later taken over by the French.	HAWS

A5834 Wt. W4973/M687 750,000 8/16 D. D. & L. Ltd. Forms/C.2118/13.

Instructions regarding War Diaries and Intelligence Summaries are contained in F. S. Regs., Part II. and the Staff Manual respectively. Title pages will be prepared in manuscript.

WAR DIARY
or
~~INTELLIGENCE~~ ~~SUMMARY~~.
(Erase heading not required.)

Army Form C. 2118.

Hqrs 40th Divisional Engineers –

Place	Date	Hour	Summary of Events and Information	Remarks and references to Appendices
RWELD	26/4/18		CRE visited CE Second Army and went round right Sector of new line. Left Sector also handed over to CRE.	HRAN
	27/4/18		CRE appointed temporarily to Command the Composite (121 Inf) Bde vice Brig General J Campbell appointed to Command 31st Division. Major PW CLARK MC assumed temporary duties of CRE. The above cancelled later to permit of CRE continuing supervision of WINNEZEELE line. 229 Fd Coy moved to SW of HERZEELE. Stats 2 off 7 OR attd 1 off 11 OR –	HAND.
	28/4/18		198 Inf Bde with 4 battn cadres moved to RWELD area to assist in supervision of Labour on new line. 121 Inf Bde left the area. 61 & 93 Labour Coy, 833 Area Employment Coy; 66, 58, 180, 181, 182 Chinese Labour Coys all under 75 Labour Group put at CRE's disposal –	HAND
	29/4/18		Above Coys moved to this area – Work continued on digging of line. 231 Fd Coy moved to S of Oudezeele. Wire & pickets drawn by 6 lorries with pontoon trailers from No 3 RE Pk Abeele.	HAND

Army Form C. 2118.

WAR DIARY
or
~~INTELLIGENCE~~ SUMMARY.

Instructions regarding War Diaries and Intelligence Summaries are contained in F. S. Regs., Part II. and the Staff Manual respectively. Title pages will be prepared in manuscript.

Hqrs 40th (Erase heading not required.) Divisional Engineers

Place	Date	Hour	Summary of Events and Information	Remarks and references to Appendices
RWELD	30/4/18		Work continued on Winnipeg line - 3 of the Chinese Labour Coys started work - Remainder moved to their respective camp sites - 833 Area Employment Coy started work under 224th Fd Coy -	HRRg

HR Ruggles-Brise
Capt RE
Adjutant 40th Div RE

A5834 Wt. W4973/M687 750,000 8/16 D. D. & L. Ltd. Forms/C.2118/13.

APP. I.

Chief Engineer,
XV Corps.

With reference to your No. 248/160 dated 13.4.18. Report on destruction of bridges over the River LYS is as follows:-

At 12-15 p.m. on the 9th inst, seeing how the situation was developing I informed all Companies that bridges were to be destroyed as the situation demanded.

(a) Cork bridge. L.30.c.35.40. This was swung to North bank and broken up at 4-0 p.m. - enemy then approaching the bridge.

(b) Pontoon bridge. G.25.d.9.4. Swung to near side and broken up at 5-45 p.m. - enemy then approaching bridge and no British troops on S. bank.

(c) Permanent bridge. G.25.d.9.4. This bridge heavily shelled all day. 1 chain to PONT LEVIS cut and 1 charge blown off. Leads cut 3 times. Last heavy transport - 2 caterpillars - crossed over bridge at 3-30 p.m.

Shortly before 5-45 p.m. a party of infantry reported enemy approaching from NOUVEAU MONDE. No British troops could be found on S. Bank and the Officer in charge tried to destroy the bridge, but the detonators only fired.

At this moment enemy approached and our troops on N. bank opened fire.

To enable the R.E. Officer to destroy the bridge the infantry recrossed the river to hold back the enemy - One circuit was refixed with new primers and detonators - the infantry were withdrawn to N.bank and a second attempt made - the detonators again alone exploded. This was at 6-15 p.m. A charge was then made up with fuze and an attempt made to destroy the lifting bridge but again only the detonators fired. Time 7-0 p.m.

(d) Cork bridge. G.26.d.23.20. - swung to near side and destroyed 3-30 p.m. - enemy then on S. bank, party under rifle fire.

(e) Cork bridge. G.26.d.80.35. - swung to near side and destroyed 3.35 p.m.-enemy then on S. bank - party under rifle fire.

(f) Pontoon bridge. G.27.c.4.4. - swung to near side and destroyed 3.40 p.m. - party under M.G. Fire.

(g) Cork bridge. G.27.a.9.0. - swung to near side and destroyed 3.45 p.m. - party under M.G. fire.

(h) Cork Bridge. G.21.d.6.3. - as (g) - destroyed at 3-50 p.m.

(j) Pontoon bridge. G.21.d.8.8. - broken up by Artillery fire -1 p.m- remainder then destroyed.

(k) Cork bridge. G.21.b.8.0. - as (g) - destroyed at 3-30 p.m.

(l) Pontoon bridge. G.16.c.7.6. - swung to N. bank 5-30 p.m. - broken up at 5-45 p.m.

(m) Permanent bridge. G.16.c.76. - effort made to fire charges 5-45 p.m. All detonators fired, but only 1 charge - one on main girders on S. end. but girder held up by cross girders - it would not however be available for heavy traffic until repaired.

The charges were then tried to be fired with fresh primers and No. 8 detonators, but again detonators alone fired.

Fresh explosives from a tool cart were then obtained and efforts made to get to the bridge at 6-45 p.m. but party unable to get there due to fire, 2 out of the party of 3 being hit.

A last effort was made at midnight but an enemy working party were found on the bridge.

(n) Pontoon bridge. G.16.b.5.5. - swung to near side and destroyed at 6-2 p.m.

(o) Permanent bridge. G.16.b.5.5.- charges blown at 6-0 p.m. - quite successful.

(p) Cork bridge. G.17.a.4.6. - as (g) - destroyed at 4-0 p.m.

(q) Cork bridge. G.17.b.40.65. - as (g) - destroyed at 4-15 p.m.

(r) Cork bridge G.18.a.25.48. - 2 remaining men of bridge party removed several sections and broke them up, but bridge was not swung.

(s) Pontoon bridge. G.18.a.9.1. - swung and destroyed 2.25.p.m. Then under rifle fire.

(t) Pontoon bridge. G.18.b.9.1. - destroyed by shell fire at 10-0a.m - remainder then broken up.

(u) Permanent bridge. G.18.b.9.1.- under fire all day - leads cut 3 times - charges fired 2-15 p.m. and demolition successful. Bridge then under rifle fire.

(v) Cork bridge. H.13.a.40.35. - as (g) - destroyed 2-30 p.m.

(w) Cork bridge. H.13.a.9.7. - as (g) - destroyed 2-30 p.m.

(x) Cork bridge. H.13.b.10.95. - as (g) - destroyed 2-35 p.m.

(y) Pontoon bridge. H.7.d.5.4. - swung and destroyed at 2-35 p.m.

(z) Cork bridge. H.7.b.75.15. - as (g) - destroyed 2.30 p.m.

Causes of failure. There seems to be no doubt that the cause of failure was due to the primers being defective.

When the Division took over on 2nd. inst, all explosives were checked in the magazines handed over - charges were fixed for practice and the amount of charges checked as to size. The magazines at Bridges G.18.b.9.1. and G.16.b.5.5. were drier and better than magazines at G.16.c.7.6. and G.25.d.9.4. which would account for the dterioration of those explosives.

Lieut.Colonel, R.E.
C.R.E. 40th. Division.

15.4.18.

Copy to 40th. Division "G"
" " O.C. 224th. Field Co. R.E.
" " O.C. 229th. Field Co. R.E.
" " O.C. 231st. Field Co. R.E.
" for War Diary.

APPENDIX II

40th Divisional R.E.

NARRATIVE OF OPERATIONS FROM 12 Midnight, 8/9th APRIL to MIDNIGHT 11/12th APRIL, 1918.

On night of 8/9th April the three Field Companies and 1 Works Company were billetted in vicinity of BAC ST MAUR. Orders were received from Division to put the emergency bridges across the River LYS at about 6-15 a.m. The bridges in Left Sector were completed at 6-45 a.m., Centre Sector 7-45 a.m., Right Sector 8-45 a.m. - in all 21 bridges extending from FORT ROMPU to ESTAIRES - permanent maintenance parties were kept on the bridges, and the remaining Sappers and Works Company were disposed for the defence of the bridgeheads in the Left and Centre Sectors - the protection of bridgeheads on the right being undertaken by another Division.

The line of the river was heavily shelled throughout the morning especially round the permanent bridges and the pontoon bridges - the Cork bridges which had been carefully hidden during construction had apparently not been detected, as they did not come in for special shelling.
About 10-30 a.m. orders were received from XVth Corps to fix charges on the permanent bridges - this was then done.
At 12-15 p.m. instructions were sent to Officers on the bridges that should the situation demand they should destroy the bridges on their own initiative without waiting for further orders.
This was acted on by the Officers concerned - the bridges being destroyed at times ranging from 2-15 p.m. at BAC ST MAUR, to 6 p.m. near SAILLY.
All bridges were destroyed at the last possible moment when they were under rifle and Machine gun fire from enemy from on S. bank of the river. Two of the pontoon bridges were destroyed earlier in the day by shell fire and the remains broken up by the Sappers.
In all 23 out of the 25 bridges were successfully destroyed along about 8,000 yards of river. The permanent bridge at SAILLY was only partially damaged by explosive and the demolition of the permanent bridge at ESTAIRES completely failed. In each case several subsequent efforts were made to carry out the demolition, but without success, as, with the exception of the one charge on SAILLY bridge none of the guncotton primers could be made to detonate.
At all the permanent bridges the leads to the charges had to be frequently repaired due to being cut by fragments of shell.
In each case after the destruction of the bridges the parties assisted in the defence of the LYS Line.

On the line going further back, on the 10th, as many of the R.E. as possible were collected with some Pioneers and attached infantry. This body was put under the command of G.O.C. 119th Brigade where they held the front line filling the gap between the 88th. Brigade and the 9th. Loyal North Lancs. N. of LE VERRIER.
They held on all day the 11th. until enfiladed from both flanks they retired 300 yards to a position 300 yards E. of LA BECQUE FARM.
At 6-30 p.m. information was received that the 31st. Division had come into the line and were about to counter attack and required a defensive flank forming. This position was taken up by the R.E. and some details of the 25th. Division - a line running approx. N. and S. 1,000 yards E. of LA BECQUE FARM - and rifle posts dug. The 31st Division went forward in front of this line, which was taken over by the D.L.I. of the 31st. Division at 11-0 p.m.

The Companies with exception of 3 Officers and about 30 men who remained with the 31st. Division till the next night - then concentrated at BAILLEUL and after a 2 hours rest proceeded to STRAZEELE reaching there the morning of the 12th.

Lieut.Colonel, R.E.

19. 4.18. C.R.E. 40th. Division.

Instructions regarding War Diaries and Intelligence Summaries are contained in F. S. Regs., Part II. and the Staff Manual respectively. Title pages will be prepared in manuscript.

Army Form C. 2118.

WAR DIARY
or
~~INTELLIGENCE SUMMARY.~~
(Erase heading not required.)

Hqrs 40th Divisional Engineers

Place	Date	Hour	Summary of Events and Information	Remarks and references to Appendices
RWELD	1/5/18		CE Second Army and VIIth Corps Commander visited these Hqrs with regard to WINNIZEELE line. 198 Bde (66th Div) left the area.	[illegible]
	2/5/18		Work continued on Winnizeele line - VIIth Corps Commander went round the line with CRE.	[illegible]
	3/5/18		Routine.	[illegible]
	4/5/18		Routine - State 2 off 10 OR Attd 12 OR	[illegible]
	5/5/18		CRE attended conference VIIth Corps Hqrs. Reconnaissance of roads between Cornhuyse & Rusch.	[illegible]
	6/5/18		The Divisional RE came under VIIth Corps as from 2nd inst. 4000x of line on the right taken over from the French. CE VIIth Corps went round the above line with CRE.	[illegible]
	7/5/18		CRE went round right sector taken over from the French. Heavy rain. Winnizeele line divided into 2 Corps Sections. 120 Bde on left and 121 Bde on right were made responsible for organization of same as regards fixing boundaries, Hqrs, dumps etc. Siting of Battery positions also delegated to Arty officers.	[illegible]

A5834 Wt. W4973/M687 750,000 8/16 D. D. & L. Ltd. Forms/C.2118/13.

Army Form C. 2118.

Instructions regarding War Diaries and Intelligence Summaries are contained in F. S. Regs., Part II. and the Staff Manual respectively. Title pages will be prepared in manuscript.

WAR DIARY
or
~~INTELLIGENCE~~ SUMMARY.
(*Erase heading not required.*)

Hqrs 40th Divisional Engineers.

Place	Date	Hour	Summary of Events and Information	Remarks and references to Appendices
RIVELD	8/5/18		GOC 40th Div & Major General Kenyon visited these Hqrs & went round a portion of the line. Major General Kenyon attached 40th DHQ to render assistance with regard to planning & construction of new lines.	HRAJ
	9/5/18		Conference held at which GOC and CREs of Sections of Winnezeele line (the) attended. CE VII Corps visited these Hqrs.	HRAJ
	10/5/18		Routine	
	11/5/18		" State 2 Off 10 OR Attd 13 OR	
	12/5/18		" Barbed wire and pickets drawn from No 2 RE Pk Renescure instead of from Abeele – 6 lorries & pontoon trailers employed as before to draw same.	HRAJ
	13/5/18		CRE went round the line with GOC 40th Div and Major General Kenyon – Certain alterations in Main Line of Resistance were agreed upon. Rained throughout the day.	HRAJ
	14/5/18		CRE went round Southern Portion Winnezeele line with GOC 40th Div and Major General Kenyon.	HRAJ

A5834 Wt. W4973/M687 750,000 8/16 D. D. & L. Ltd. Forms/C.2118/13.

Army Form C. 2118.

WAR DIARY
or
~~INTELLIGENCE SUMMARY.~~
(Erase heading not required.)

Hqrs 40th Divisional Engineers

* Instructions regarding War Diaries and Intelligence Summaries are contained in F. S. Regs., Part II. and the Staff Manual respectively. Title pages will be prepared in manuscript.

Place	Date	Hour	Summary of Events and Information	Remarks and references to Appendices
RWELD	15/5/18		Routine	[illegible]
	16/5/18		"	[illegible]
	17/5/18		CRE met officers of Sector on Right to arrange coordination of trench system at boundary of Sectors.	[illegible]
	18/5/18		Sites for Corps & Divisional RE dumps in Left Section (Wemmysale Line) Reconnoitred – State 2 Off 10 OR Attd 10 OR.	
	19/5/18		Routine –	[illegible]
	20/5/18		Trenches in Right Corps Section named –	[illegible] [illegible]
	21/5/18		CRE met GOC 40th Div on right boundary –	[illegible]
	22/5/18		General Kenyon went round the line with CRE –	[illegible]
	23/5/18		Routine	[illegible]

A5834 Wt. W4973/M687 750,000 8/16 D. D. & L. Ltd. Forms/C.2118/13.

Instructions regarding War Diaries and Intelligence Summaries are contained in F. S. Regs., Part II. and the Staff Manual respectively. Title pages will be prepared in manuscript.

WAR DIARY
or
~~INTELLIGENCE SUMMARY.~~
(Erase heading not required.)

Hqrs 40th Divisional Engineers

Army Form C. 2118.

Place	Date	Hour	Summary of Events and Information	Remarks and references to Appendices
RWEZD	24/5/18		CRE went round trenches in Hazebrouck area with General Kenyon –	HWG
	25/5/18		2 Sections 231 Fd Coy moved to neighbourhood of St Sylvestre Cappel for work under CRE No 1 Sector – Decision made that Support line to Main line of Resistance & Reserve Line should not be dug. State 2 off 10 OR Att'd 11 OR –	HWG
	26/5/18		Routine.	HWG
	27/5/18		Routine.	
	28/5/18		CRE met GOC 40th Div & reconnoitred ground for siting of the new Caestre Line, midway between the Winnezeele line & St Omer defences – He later accompanied VIIth Corps Commander round the Winnezeele Line –	HWG
	29/5/18		Routine. 66 Chinese Labour Coy left the area –	HWG
	30/5/18		CRE met GOC 40th Div & went over proposed Caestre Line –	HWG

D. D. & L., London, E.C.
(A8004) Wt. W1771/M2 31 750,000 5/17 Sch. 52 Forms/C2118/14

Army Form C. 2118.

Instructions regarding War Diaries and Intelligence Summaries are contained in F. S. Regs., Part II. and the Staff Manual respectively. Title pages will be prepared in manuscript.

WAR DIARY
or
~~INTELLIGENCE SUMMARY~~.
(Erase heading not required.)

Hqrs 40th Divisional Engineers —

Place	Date	Hour	Summary of Events and Information	Remarks and references to Appendices
RIVELD	31/5/18		Routine – 58 CLC left the area for work on L of C.	HRRD

H R Ruggles-Brise Capt RE
for CRE 40th Div
31/5/18

D. D. & L., London, E.C. (A8004) Wt. W1771/M2 31 750,000 5/17 Sch. 52 Forms/C2118/14

Instructions regarding War Diaries and Intelligence Summaries are contained in F. S. Regs., Part II. and the Staff Manual respectively. Title pages will be prepared in manuscript.

WAR DIARY
or
~~INTELLIGENCE SUMMARY.~~
(Erase heading not required.)

Army Form C. 2118.

Hqrs 40th Divl Engineers

Place	Date	Hour	Summary of Events and Information	Remarks and references to Appendices
RWELD	1/6/18		Work continued on the Wemmigele Line – CRE met GOC 40th Div & reconnoitred Balemberg Line – State 2 Off 7 OR – Attd 11. OR –	HRWS
	2/6/18		Routine – Reconnaissance of Balemberg Line by CRE & Coy Commanders and fixing of Camp Sites.	HRWS
	3/6/18		Hqrs & 2 Sections of both 224 and 229 Fd Coys proceeded to Camp sites at Balemberg and North of Rubrouck respectively to start work on Balemberg Line. 93 Labour Coy, 833 Area Employment & 182 Chinese Labour Coy also proceeded to that area – CRE went round the Balemberg Line with Corps Commander XVth Corps –	HRWS
DOORNAERT	4/6/18		Hqrs RE moved to DOORNAERT near RUBROUCK – Work started on the Balemberg Line –	HRWS
	5/6/18		Work continued –	HRWS
	6/6/18		Lt Col AC Baylay DSO, CRE 40th Div appointed to Command 59th Inf Bde and proceeded to assume duties – Major FW Clarke MC (229 Fd Coy RE) assumed duties of acting CRE.	HRWS

D. D. & L., London, E.C.
(A8004) Wt. W1771/M2 31 750,000 5/17 Sch. 52 Forms/C2118/14

Army Form C. 2118.

WAR DIARY
or
INTELLIGENCE SUMMARY.
(*Erase heading not required.*)

Instructions regarding War Diaries and Intelligence Summaries are contained in F. S. Regs., Part II. and the Staff Manual respectively. Title pages will be prepared in manuscript.

Place	Date	Hour	Summary of Events and Information	Remarks and references to Appendices
DOORNAERT	7/6/18		CRE met GOC 120 Inf Bde & laid out Reserve Line left Sector 1st Middlesex Labour Company arrived for work under 224 Fd Coy –	HRNS
	8/6/18		CRE met GOC 121 Inf Bde & laid out Reserve Line Rgt Sector – 181 CLC moved back for work on Balemberg Line under 224 Fd Coy – Staff 2 off 7 OR. CHd 2 off. 13 OR –	HRNS
	9/6/18		231 Fd Coy complete moved to S of Hondeghem for work on wiring under CRE No 1 Sector –	
	10/6/18		Detached Sections of 224 Fd Coy rejoined their Coy at BALEMBERG –	HRNS
	11/6/18		Detached Sections of 229 Fd Coy rejoined their Coy North of Riebroeck 150 CLC moved back for work on Balemberg Line under 229 Fd Coy.	HRNS
	12/6/18		Alteration & resiting of Main Line of Resistance in Southern portion of Balemberg line –	HRNS
	13/6/18		Routine – Chinese Festival – Consequent upon which Chinese Labour Coys had a holiday. half the Coys on one day, half on the next.	
	14/6/18		CRE met General Kenyon and laid out Reserve Line –	HRNS

D. D. & L., London, E.C.
(A8004) Wt. W1771/M2 31 750,000 5/17 Sch. 52 Forms/C2118/14

Instructions regarding War Diaries and Intelligence Summaries are contained in F. S. Regs., Part II. and the Staff Manual respectively. Title pages will be prepared in manuscript.

Army Form C. 2118.

WAR DIARY

or

~~INTELLIGENCE SUMMARY.~~

(Erase heading not required.)

Hqrs 40th Divisional Engineers

Place	Date	Hour	Summary of Events and Information	Remarks and references to Appendices
DOORNAERE	15/6/18		Lt Col R P Pakenham-Walsh MC RE assumed duties of CRE 40th Div — Major F R Clark MC RE returned to 229 Fd Coy RE. Orders received for 224 and 231 Fd Coys to man the Hazebrouck Line in the event of an enemy offensive in that area — State 2 off 7 OR — Attd 1 off. 11 OR —	HAWS —
	16/6/18		Routine — Siting of Artillery OP's on Winnezeele Line with BG H Cory Arty VIIth Corps — Orders received for 229 Fd Coy also to man the W Hazebrouck Line in case of necessity —	HAWS
	17/6/18		Routine — Siting of OP's continued —	HAWS
	18/6/18		CRE met General Kenyon & went into the siting of trenches around Noordpeene —	HAWS
	19/6/18		Routine —	HAWS
	20/6/18		Reconnaissance of sites for blowing craters in roads in front of the Winnezeele Line —	HAWS
	21/6/18		Routine —	HAWS
	22/6/18		" State 2 off 7 OR Attd 10 OR —	HAWS

D. D. & L., London, E.C. (A8004) Wt. W1771/M2 31 750,000 5/17 Sch. 52 Forms/C2118/14

Instructions regarding War Diaries and Intelligence Summaries are contained in F. S. Regs., Part II. and the Staff Manual respectively. Title pages will be prepared in manuscript.

WAR DIARY
or
~~INTELLIGENCE SUMMARY.~~

Army Form C. 2118.

Hqrs 40th (Erase heading not required.) Divisional Engineers

Place	Date	Hour	Summary of Events and Information	Remarks and references to Appendices
RENESCURE	23/6/18		Hqrs RE rejoined Div HQ at Renescure.	
			224 Fd Coy took over work from 207 Fd Coy & moved to NE of Wallon Cappel	
			229 " " " " 236 AT Coy " " N of Sercus –	
			All work on Balemberg & Wannygale Lines handed over to Lt Col Close RE.	
			All work on W Hazebrouck Lines taken over from Lt Col Close RE.	HRRS
	24/6/18		Routine – CRE & General Kenyon went round the W Hazebrouck Line –	
			Labour for work on W Hazebrouck line supplied by 5th Labour Group – RE Stores drawn from Renescure by 12 lorries, put at CRE's disposal –	HRRS
	25/6/18		In the event of an attack on the Hazebrouck Line 224, 229, 231 Fd Coys, 236 AT Coy, 234 Fd Coy, 537 & 214 AT Coys, 207 Fd Coy will form a Divisional reserve under CRE.	HRRS
	26/6/18		Routine.	HRRS
	27/6/18		Practice Assembly of RE Coys in Divisional Reserve near Ebblinghem.	HRRS.
	28/6/18		Routine. Conference of Brigadiers, Bde majors, CRE & adjt at DHQ. Work started on 2 Rifle Ranges –	HRRS
	29/6/18		Routine – State 20 off 7 OR att'd 35 OR (to include lorry drivers).	HRRS
	30/6/18		CRE inspected 224 & 231 Fd Coys on parade –	HRRS

HRRuggles-Brise
Capt RE adjt 40th Div Engineers – 1/7/18

D. D. & L., London, E.C.
(A8004) Wt. W1771/M2 31 750,000 5/17 Sch. 52 Forms/C2118/14

Instructions regarding War Diaries and Intelligence Summaries are contained in F. S. Regs., Part II. and the Staff Manual respectively. Title pages will be prepared in manuscript.

WAR DIARY
or
~~INTELLIGENCE SUMMARY.~~

Army Form C. 2118.

Hqrs 40th (*Erase heading not required.*) Divisional Engineers –

Place	Date	Hour	Summary of Events and Information	Remarks and references to Appendices
RENESCURE	1/7/18		Work continued on the West Hazebrouck Line – Construction of Rifle Ranges by 224 & 229 Fd Coys –	HAWS
	2/7/18		Routine	AWS
	3/7/18		CRE reconnoitred houses on the W. Hazebrouck Line which required to be demolished by reason of obstructing Field of Fire – Major General J Ponsonby left to assume duties of GOC 5th Division & was succeeded by Major General Sir WE Peyton.	HAWS –
	4/7/18		Repairs effected to Rifle Range at La Belle Hotesse by 229 Fd Coy –	
			Routine	HAWS
	5/7/18		"	HAWS
	6/7/18		Hqrs RE & 224, 229, 231 Fd Coys transferred to XVth Corps – CRE went round OP's on W. Hazebrouck Line with Genl Metcalfe BGHA XV Corps. State 2 off 7 OR. Attd 15 OR.	HAWS
	7/7/18		CRE inspected 229 Fd Coy on parade – CRE accompanied Lt Colonel Butler CRE Southern Sector round Southern portion of W Hazebrouck Line with view to taking over same. 164 Labour Coy transferred from 231 to 229 Fd Coy Sector for work. 13 " " " " " " 224 " " " " "	HAWS

D. D. & L., London, E.C. (A8004) Wt. W1771/M2 31 750,000 5/17 Sch. 52 Forms/C2118/14

Army Form C. 2118.

WAR DIARY
or
~~INTELLIGENCE SUMMARY.~~
(Erase heading not required.)

Hqrs 40th Divisional Engineers

Instructions regarding War Diaries and Intelligence Summaries are contained in F. S. Regs., Part II. and the Staff Manual respectively. Title pages will be prepared in manuscript.

Place	Date	Hour	Summary of Events and Information	Remarks and references to Appendices
RENESCURE	8/7/18		Routine – CRE went round the line with CE XVth Corps – CE VIIth Corps visited these Hqrs –	[initials]
	9/7/18		Routine –	[initials]
	10/7/18		Wannyvale Line from Bois des Huits Rues handed over to CRE St Omer Defences – Morbecque Switch & Romarin Reserve Line taken over from CRE St Omer Defences –	[initials]
	11/7/18		Routine – 224 Fd Coy moved to SE of St Sylvestre Cappel for work under CRE Le Peuplier Sector. 174 Labour Coy came under 229 Fd Coy for work.	[initials]
	12/7/18		Routine	[initials]
	13/7/18		{ CRE met CE Second Army & went round W Hazebrouck Line. State 2 off. 7. OR. att 2 off 11. OR.	[initials]
	14/7/18		Routine.	[initials]
	15/7/18		Lt Col R Pakenham-Walsh MC RE left to assume duties (temporarily) of CRE 3rd Division – Major J E Villa MC RE (231 Fd Coy) assumed duties temporarily of CRE 40th Div.	[initials]

D. D. & L., London, E.C.
(A8094) Wt. W1771/M2 31 750,000 5/17 Sch. 52 Forms/C2118/14

Instructions regarding War Diaries and Intelligence Summaries are contained in F. S. Regs., Part II. and the Staff Manual respectively. Title pages will be prepared in manuscript.

WAR DIARY
or
~~INTELLIGENCE SUMMARY.~~

Army Form C. 2118.

Hqrs 40th (Erase heading not required.) Divisional Engineers

Place	Date	Hour	Summary of Events and Information	Remarks and references to Appendices
RENESCURE	16/7/18		Routine	HARRIS
	17/7/18		"	HARRIS
	18/7/18		GOC 40th Div inspected 231 and 229 Fd Coy's Camps.	HARRIS
	19/7/18		CRE went round proposed Bde and Battn Hqrs W Hazebrouck Line with view to selecting sites for Concrete Pill Boxes for Telephone Exchanges.	HARRIS
	20/7/18		Routine – State 1 off 6 OR Attd 3 off 19 OR.	HARRIS
	21/7/18		Church Parade held at which 1 section of 229 Fd Coy attended; 120 Inf Bde, 121 Inf Bde, RAMC, 17th Worcester Regt Pioneers, ASC personnel on parade. 40th Divisional RE Sports held in the afternoon 1 mile S of Hondeghem, at which the Divisional Commander and the Acting CE XVth Corps were present.	HARRIS
	22/7/18		CRE showed OC 3rd Canadian Tunnelling Coy round sites selected for Block Pill Boxes.	HARRIS
	23/7/18		94th & 111th Labour Coys ceased to be employed under 40th Div RE.	HARRIS
	24/7/18		CRE went round OP's.	HARRIS.

D. D. & L., London, E.C.
(A8004) Wt. W1771/M2 31 750,000 5/17 Sch. 52 Forms/C2118/14

Instructions regarding War Diaries and Intelligence Summaries are contained in F. S. Regs., Part II. and the Staff Manual respectively. Title pages will be prepared in manuscript.

WAR DIARY
or
~~INTELLIGENCE SUMMARY.~~

Army Form C. 2118.

Hqrs 40th (*Erase heading not required.*) Divisional Engineers

Place	Date	Hour	Summary of Events and Information	Remarks and references to Appendices
RENESCURE	25/7/18		61 Labour Coy ceased to be employed on W. Hazebrouck Line, under CRE.	HAMJ
	26/7/18		CE XV Corps visited these Hqrs. 174 Labour Coy ceased to be employed under CRE on W. Hazebrouck Line.	HAMJ
	27/7/18		CRE went round new MG emplacements. State. 1 off. 7 OR. att^d 2 off. 17 OR.	HAMJ
	28/7/18		Routine	HAMJ
	29/7/18		CRE went round MG emplacements & fortified houses. 17th Worc Regt Pioneers started work on W Hazebrouck Line.	HAMJ
	30/7/18		Routine. The Div^l Commander inspected 40th Div Signal Coy on parade. (Hqrs & No 1 Section only).	HAMJ
	31/7/18		Routine. 132 Labour Coy ceased work under CRE on W Hazebrouck Line.	HAMJ

H R Ruggles-Brise
Capt RE
Adjutant
40th Div^l Engineers 31/7/18

D. D. & L., London, E.C.
(A10266) Wt W5300/P713 750,000 2/18 Sch. 52 Forms/C2118/16

Army Form C. 2118.

Instructions regarding War Diaries and Intelligence Summaries are contained in F. S. Regs., Part II. and the Staff Manual respectively. Title pages will be prepared in manuscript.

WAR DIARY
or
~~INTELLIGENCE SUMMARY.~~

Hqrs 40th (*Erase heading not required.*) Divisional Engineers –

Place	Date	Hour	Summary of Events and Information	Remarks and references to Appendices
RENESCURE	1/8/18		Work continued on W Hazebrouck Line – 12, 13, 164 Labour Coys ceased to be employed under CRE 40th on being transferred for work to E Hazebrouck Line. 224 Fd Coy continued to work under CRE Le Peuplier Switch.	HRWS
	2/8/18		Routine.	HRWS
	3/8/18		CRE went round right (extreme boundary) of W Hazebrouck Line. State 1 off 6 OR – Att'd 2 off. 17 OR.	HRWS
	4/8/18		A/Lt Col W R Wilson MC RE (from 23rd Field Coy) assumed duties of CRE 40th Div, Lt Col R Pakenham Walsh MC RE having been confirmed in the ~~appointment of CRE~~ 3rd Division. Major J E Villa MC RE (231 Fd Coy) ceased to act as CRE 40th Div – XV Corps Reinforcement Batt'n arrived for work under 231 Fd Coy. Parade Service held to commemorate 4th Anniversary of the beginning of the War at which all units in the 2nd Army were represented.	HRWS
	5/8/18		Routine – Portion of the line near left boundary handed over to CRE Le Peuplier Switch.	HRWS
	6/8/18		Routine	
	7/8/18		CRE went round right Sector.	HRWS

D. D. & L., London, E.C.
(A8004) Wt. W1771/M2 31 750,000 5/17 Sch. 52 Forms/C2118/14

Army Form C. 2118.

WAR DIARY
or
~~INTELLIGENCE~~ ~~SUMMARY.~~
(Erase heading not required.)

Instructions regarding War Diaries and Intelligence Summaries are contained in F. S. Regs., Part II. and the Staff Manual respectively. Title pages will be prepared in manuscript.

Agra 40th Div^l Engineers

Place	Date	Hour	Summary of Events and Information	Remarks and references to Appendices
RENESCURE	8/8/18		Routine	HAMS
	9/8/18		CRE attended lecture by the Inspector General of Training and demonstration afterwards. XV Corps Reinforcement Batt^n left the area & ceased to be employed.	HAMS
	10/8/18		CRE took CE XV Corps round the W. Hazebrouck Line.	HAMS
	11/8/18		Parade service held at which the King was present. Units of Second Army were represented on parade. State 2 off. 7 OR att^d 1 off 16 OR.	HAMS
	12/8/18		Routine.	
	13/8/18		CRE went round sites for more Pill boxes for MG Emplacements with OC 3rd Canadian Tunnelling Coy.	HAMS
	14/8/18		Routine.	HAMS
	15/8/18		CRE inspected new scheme devised by 224 Fd Coy for closing gaps in wire & visited 224 & 231 Coy Hqrs. 231 Fd Coy started work on E Hazebrouck Line under CRE XV Corps Troops.	HAMS
	16/8/18		Routine.	HAMS
	17/8/18		State 2 off 6 OR. att^d 1 off 22 OR	HAMS

D. D. & L., London, E.C.
(A10266) Wt W5300/P713 750,000 2/18 Sch. 52 Forms/C2118/16

Army Form C. 2118.

WAR DIARY
or
INTELLIGENCE SUMMARY.
(*Erase heading not required.*)

Instructions regarding War Diaries and Intelligence Summaries are contained in F. S. Regs., Part II. and the Staff Manual respectively. Title pages will be prepared in manuscript.

Hqrs 40th Divisional Engineers

Place	Date	Hour	Summary of Events and Information	Remarks and references to Appendices
RENESCURE	18/8/18		Selection of sites for Winter Camps – 231 Fd Coy, 12, 13, 132 Labour Coys resumed work on W Hazebrouck Line.	HAMS –
	19/8/18		Div. Horse Show held at which RE units competed.	HAMS
	20/8/18		Routine.	HAMS
	21/8/18		CRE met CRE 31 Div & went round the line with a view to taking over.	HAMS
near WALLON-CAPPEL	22/8/18		Divisional Hqrs (less Artillery Hqrs) moved to near Wallon-Cappel in relief of 31st Div in the line – Div. Dump near Wallon-Cappel taken over from 31st Div – Personnel employed:– 3 RE, 30 Pioneers or Infantry.	HAMS
	23/8/18		229 Fd Coy relieved 223 Fd Coy in Rgt Sector and 231 Fd Coy relieved 210 Fd Coy in reserve both Coys located South of Hazebrouck – The Division carried out a minor operation advancing their line towards Neuf Berquin. 5 OR of Forestry Coy No 362 worked on cutting pickets in Bois D'Aval under 229 Fd Coy. A detachment 196 Land Drainage Coy employed on drainage –	HAMS
	24/8/18		224 Fd Coy relieved 211 Fd Coy in Left Sector – State 2 off 5 OR. Attd. 1 off 10 OR a detachment 3rd Canadian Tunnelling Coy worked on concrete shelters in the Div. Area –	HAMS
	25/8/18		17th Worcester Bn Pioneers relieved 12th KOYLI Pioneers – Chief work in hand by RE & Pioneers is maintenance & repair of roads & bridges consequent upon the enemy withdrawing –	HAMS –

D. D. & L., London, E.C. (A8001) Wt. W1771/M2 31 750,000 5/17 Sch. 52 Forms/C2118/14

Instructions regarding War Diaries and Intelligence Summaries are contained in F. S. Regs., Part II. and the Staff Manual respectively. Title pages will be prepared in manuscript.

WAR DIARY
or
INTELLIGENCE SUMMARY.
(*Erase heading not required.*)

Army Form C. 2118.

Place	Date	Hour	Summary of Events and Information	Remarks and references to Appendices
near WALLON-CAPPEL	26/8/18		Routine – Selection of new site for Div.l dump at La Souverain & removal of stores thereto. Work & supervision of W Hazebrouck Line handed over to CRE 9th Div –	HAMS
	27/8/18		119 Inf Bde attacked & advanced their line SE of Vieux Berquin – RE & Pioneers chiefly employed on repair of roads, bridges & making of tracks –	HAMS
	28/8/18		CRE went round roads in forward area –	HAMS
	29/8/18		Routine – The 120 Inf Bde advanced their line by a successful minor operation on the Right Sector	HAMS
	30/8/18		CRE went round left sector of Divisional front. The enemy continued to withdraw –	HAMS
	31/8/18		Routine –	
			State 2 O [illegible] 40 OR att.d 1 O 11 OR	HAMS

D. D. & L., London, E.C.
(A10266) Wt W5300/P713 750,000 2/15 Sch. 52 Forms/C2118/16

H R Ruggles-Brise Capt
Adjt 40th Divisional Engineers

Army Form C. 2118.

Instructions regarding War Diaries and Intelligence Summaries are contained in F. S. Regs., Part II. and the Staff Manual respectively. Title pages will be prepared in manuscript.

WAR DIARY

or

~~INTELLIGENCE SUMMARY~~.

(*Erase heading not required.*) Hqrs 40th Divisional Engineers

Place	Date	Hour	Summary of Events and Information	Remarks and references to Appendices
Nr WALLON-CAPPEL	1/9/18		CRE went round the line with CE XV Corps – Detachment of 196 Land Drainage Coy ceased to be employed in 40th Divl. area. Field Coys & Pioneers employed chiefly on repair of roads & bridges – Detachment of 3rd Canadian Tunnelling Coy employed on investigating & removing enemy mines & traps –	[illegible]
LA MOTTE.	2/9/18		229 Fd Coy moved to neighbourhood of Vieux Berquin – Hqrs RE moved with DHQ to La Motte – 3 sections of 224 Fd Coy moved to forward area. Line advanced through Croix du Bac –	[illegible]
	3/9/18		229 Fd Coy moved to Le Verrier –	[illegible]
	4/9/18		Routine – Hqrs & Transport of 224 Fd Coy moved to forward area.	[illegible]
	5/9/18		The line was again advanced, Fd Coys & Pioneers engaged on repair of roads & bridges.	[illegible]
	6/9/18		Routine.	[illegible]
	7/9/18		The 119 Inf Bde took part in an attack on the left front. 229 Fd Coy moved to S of Steenwerck. Strength Offs 2 OR 7. attached Off 1 OR 11	[illegible]

D. D. & L., London, E.C.
(A10266) W1 W5300/P713 750,000 2/18 Sch. 52 Forms/C2118/16

Army Form C. 2118.

WAR DIARY
or
~~INTELLIGENCE SUMMARY.~~

Instructions regarding War Diaries and Intelligence Summaries are contained in F. S. Regs., Part II. and the Staff Manual respectively. Title pages will be prepared in manuscript.

Hqrs 40th Divisional Engineers –

(Erase heading not required.)

Place	Date	Hour	Summary of Events and Information	Remarks and references to Appendices
LA MOTTE	8/9/18		Routine –	HAMS
	9/9/18		224 Fd Coy moved to location East of Steenwerck – Transport remained W of Steenwerck –	HAMS
	10/9/18		231 Fd Coy (less 2 sections) moved to near Doulieu –	HAMS
	11/9/18		Routine –	HAMS
	12/9/18		"	HAMS
	13/9/18		– Coys employed on improving Nieppe System, repairing billets, erecting baths, road repair, salving RE material – Pioneers on road repair –	HAMS
	14/9/18		Routine – Strength off 2 or 8 attached off 1 or 11	HAMS
	15/9/18		"	HAMS
	16/9/18		"	HAMS

D. D. & L., London, E.C.
(A10266) Wt W5300/P713 750,000 2/18 Sch. 52 Forms/C2118/16

Instructions regarding War Diaries and Intelligence Summaries are contained in F. S. Regs., Part II. and the Staff Manual respectively. Title pages will be prepared in manuscript.

WAR DIARY
or
~~INTELLIGENCE SUMMARY.~~
(Erase heading not required.)

Army Form C. 2118.

Hqrs 40th Div'l Engineers –

Place	Date	Hour	Summary of Events and Information	Remarks and references to Appendices
LA MOTTE	17/9/18		System of getting RE Stores forward was by lorry from old Div'l dump South of Hazebrouck to a dump W of Steenwerck – Stores were also delivered to Bailleul by rail and collected from there by lorry – Considerable quantities of stores were salved – 4 lorries FWD with trailers employed daily on conveying stores forward and more lorries when available.	
			No 47906 RSM A C Cook RE proceeded to England to take up the appointment of Qmr. RE with rank of Lieutenant –	HMD
	18/9/18		CRE went round the posts in the Nieppe System –	HMD
			A platoon of 17 Battn Worcester Regt Pioneers employed on making duckboards in Nieppe Forest.	
	19/9/18		Routine	EW
	20/9/18		Routine adjutant proceeded on leave. Lieut E W[illegible] RE a/adjutant	EW
	21/9/18		Routine Strength off 1 or 9 attached off 2 or 33	
	22/9/18		CRE arranged site for new Div'l HQ + consulted with CRE 31st Div with reference to taking over addition to Divisional Area	EW

D. D. & L., London, E.C.
(A10266) Wt W3300/P713 750,000 2/18 Sch. 52 Forms/C2118/16

Army Form C. 2118.

Instructions regarding War Diaries and Intelligence Summaries are contained in F. S. Regs., Part II. and the Staff Manual respectively. Title pages will be prepared in manuscript.

WAR DIARY
or
INTELLIGENCE SUMMARY.
(Erase heading not required.)

Place	Date	Hour	Summary of Events and Information	Remarks and references to Appendices
LA MOTTE	23/9/18		STEERNWERCK STATION Dump taken over from CRE 31st Div Routine	EW
	24/9/18		STEENWERCK STATION DUMP returned to CRE 31st DIV Routine	EW
	25/9/18		MAJ J.E. VILLA returned from Special Leave & took over command of 231st Field Co from Capt E J Dowson RE	EW
	26/9/18		Routine STEENWERCK Station Dump again taken over from 31st Div Companies improving NIEPPE System Building new Dvl H.Q. Baths etc	EW EW
	27/9/18		Routine Strength Off. 1 OR 9 attached Off. 2 OR 29	EW
	28/9/18		Routine Companies Screening Front Line Trenches	EW
	29/9/18		Routine	EW
	30/9/18		CRE Head Quarters moved to A 21 b 2.8. Sheet 36 N.W	

D. D. & L., London, E.C.
(A10266) Wt W5300/P713 750,000 2/18 Sch. 52 Forms/C2118/16

Instructions regarding War Diaries and Intelligence Summaries are contained in F. S. Regs., Part II. and the Staff Manual respectively. Title pages will be prepared in manuscript.

WAR DIARY
or
~~INTELLIGENCE SUMMARY.~~
(Erase heading not required.)

Army Form C. 2118.

Hqrs 40th Divl Engineers

Place	Date	Hour	Summary of Events and Information	Remarks and references to Appendices
1 mile N of STEENWERCK	1/10/18		In anticipation of a further advance Bridge sites had been selected at H2c28 and H3c47 across the Lys – Pontoons were kept loaded on wagons at a convenient distance and work was proceeding on the approach road to H3c47 past Gospel Villa –	HMS
	2/10/18		In the morning a daylight reconnaissance was being made from GOSPEL Villa Eastwards along the LYS towards ERQUINGHEM when at 12.00 hours patrols of the 61st Div on our right were observed feeling their way through the village – Orders were immediately given to bridge the river and by 15.15 hours the Pontoon bridge at H3c47 was completed – The other bridges were completed by 17.00 hours the same evening viz (1) Pontoon at H2c28 (2) Barrel Pier bridge at H3d54 (3) Footbridge at H4c14	
			Average width of river was about 80' but at each Pontoon site advantage was taken of partly demolished landing stages left by the enemy. Approaches to both these bridges were only fair but the west bridge had an excellent slab road on the North Bank – These approaches were improved during the succeeding days –	
			Bridging was being carried on simultaneously on Left Bde front N of Armentières where no previous reconnaissance was possible. Infantry of this Bde was holding	

D. D. & L., London, E.C.
(A10266) Wt W5300/P713 750,000 2/18 Sch. 52 Forms/C2118/16

Instructions regarding War Diaries and Intelligence Summaries are contained in F. S. Regs., Part II. and the Staff Manual respectively. Title pages will be prepared in manuscript.

WAR DIARY
or
~~INTELLIGENCE~~ SUMMARY.
(*Erase heading not required.*)

Hqrs 40th Div Engineers

Army Form C. 2118.

Place	Date	Hour	Summary of Events and Information	Remarks and references to Appendices
1 mile W of STEENWERCK	2/10/18 cont^d		till a Cork Foot Bridge was constructed at C15d68 on the night of 2nd/3rd Oct. Material for this was ready but great difficulty was experienced in getting wagons forward owing to the bad condition of roads – Actually it had to be carried 600 yds to the River and the Infantry crossed by 03.00 hrs	HAMS
	3/10/18		A ferry was improvised and used at C19c78 by 6 am for passage of troops. Work on forward roads & craters continued.	HAMS
	4/10/18		Two more pontoon bridges were completed by the evening – one at NOUVEL HOUPLINES C20d9.0 the other at ERQUINGHEM H4c14. 2 weldon trestles & 3 pontoons having been obtained from 9th Pontoon Pk after much difficulty for this purpose. The Northern approach to H4c14 was in excellent condition but the Southern side of the river was blocked by tons of debris which took considerable clearing. Other footbridges were constructed in C21a & b utilizing intact lock gates. 224 Fd Coy carried out the work at H3c47, H3d54, H4c15 229 [illegible] H2c28, H4c14 231 [illegible] North of Armentieres	HAMS

D. D. & L., London, E.C.
(A10266) Wt W5300/P713 750,000 2/18 Sch. 52 Forms/C2118/16

Instructions regarding War Diaries and Intelligence Summaries are contained in F. S. Regs., Part II. and the Staff Manual respectively. Title pages will be prepared in manuscript.

WAR DIARY
or
~~INTELLIGENCE SUMMARY.~~

Army Form C. 2118.

H Q 40th Divl Engineers (Erase heading not required.)

Place	Date	Hour	Summary of Events and Information	Remarks and references to Appendices
1 mile W of STEENWERCK	5/10/18		Footbridge at Houplines completed – weekly strength 1 off. 7 or. attached 2 off. 11 or.	HAMS
	6/10/18		229 Fd Coy moved to ERQUINGHEM and 231 Fd Coy to SE of ERQUINGHEM	HAMS
	7/10/18		Routine	
	8/10/18		½ No 1 Chinese Labour Coy arrived at Steenwerck for work in the Div Area chiefly the repair of houses in Steenwerck.	HAMS
	9/10/18		Routine –	HAMS
	10/10/18		"	
	11/10/18			HAMS
	12/10/18		weekly strength 2 off. 7 or. attached 1 off. 10 or.	HAMS
	13/10/18			

D. D. & L., London, E.C.
(A10266) Wt W5300/P713 750,000 2/18 Sch. 52 Forms/C2118/16

Instructions regarding War Diaries and Intelligence Summaries are contained in F. S. Regs., Part II. and the Staff Manual respectively. Title pages will be prepared in manuscript.

WAR DIARY
or
~~INTELLIGENCE~~ SUMMARY.

H Q 40th (Erase heading not required.) Divl Engineers

Army Form C. 2118.

Place	Date	Hour	Summary of Events and Information	Remarks and references to Appendices
1 mile W of STEENWERCK	14/10/18		Pontoon Bridge over River LYS at H2 c1.9 dismantled & loaded in readiness for a further advance work on New Divisional H.Qrs ARMENTIERES.	EW
			Capt HR Ruggles-Brise Adjt RE attached for duty with General Staff 40th Div Lt E. Willborn RE assumed duty as acting Adjutant	EW
	15/10/18		Routine	
	16/10/18		40th Division having advanced their line in the direction towards QUESNOY & PERENCHIES. Field Coys moved forward. 224th Field Coy RE to ARMENTIERES B30 c 4.1. 229th Field Coy RE to CHAPELLE & D'ARMENTIERES 231st FIELD COY RE to HOUPLINES C27 a 1.8.	EW
			At daybreak a party of 231st Field Coy RE went out with Infantry Patrols & proceeded further forward to work on filling in Crater at C30 central to facilitate advance.	EW
		3pm	40th Div line reported on line approx N & S. C30 central & still advancing	
	17/10/18		Field Coys following up the retreating enemy & preparing roads for Transport. Unexploded mine removed from PERENCHIES J14 a 9.9. Deviations made round Craters at LA CROIX, D29 b 5.5, D30 a 2.9 D24 c 5.3 & WAMBRECHIES	EW
			Pontoon Bridge C20 d 8.1 dismantled & handed over to 14th Div 231st Field Coy moved to J1 b 7.7.	EW
	18/10/18		Pontoon Bridge H3 c 4.7 dismantled & conveyed to WAMBRECHIES. Making deviations round Craters. Bridges commenced C30 d 9.10. D24 c 7.7. Reconnaissances of Roads & Bridges made up to ROUBAIX.	EW
			40th Divl H.Q. moved to ARMENTIERES CRE's HQ & Mess at 21 JAEGER St ARMENTIERES.	EW

D. D. & L., London, E.C.
(A10266) Wt W5300/P713 750,000 2/18 Sch. 52 Forms/C2118/16

Instructions regarding War Diaries and Intelligence Summaries are contained in F. S. Regs., Part II. and the Staff Manual respectively. Title pages will be prepared in manuscript.

WAR DIARY
or
~~INTELLIGENCE SUMMARY~~.

Army Form C. 2118.

H.Q. 40th (*Erase heading not required.*) Divl Engineers

Place	Date	Hour	Summary of Events and Information	Remarks and references to Appendices
ARMENTIERES	19/10/18	14.30	Two Bridges over destroyed culverts at C 30 d. 9.0 had been converted to carry 10 tons Axle Load	EW
		06.00	Bridge over La Basse Deule River at WAMBRECHIES had been erected to take 12 tons Axle Load	
			all available labour was turned on to roads making diversions round large craters & a through Lorry route was made passable from ARMENTIERES to ROUBAIX	
			Bridges to take Field Guns were completed at L 8 a 5.2 & L 2 d. 3.5. also a causeway at F 22. b 0.3	
			weekly strength 1 off. 6 or. attached 3 off 36 or	
MOUVAUX	20/10/18		40th Div H.Q. removed to MOUVAUX & CRE's H.Q. office opened at 185 Rue de ROUBAIX	EW
			Bridges completed for Field Guns at D 24 d 0.7 & work was in progress strengthening Bridge at WAMBRECHIES & making a Bridge to take Lorries at F 27. b 9.9.	
	21/10/18		work continued on forward Roads & Bridging Lorry Route made good & open from ARMENTIERES to MOUVAUX	EW
			Pontoon Bridge over River LYS at ERQUINGHEM H 4 c 1 4 dismantled & sent forward to MOUVAUX	
	22/10/18		Bridge at L 8 a 5.2 PLOMEUX LOCK completed to take 21 tons Axle Load	EW
			" " F 27 b 9.9 strengthened & completed to take Lorries 8 tons Axle Load	
			Clearing commenced to make Road into ROUBAIX through Railway Embankment at F 29 a 0.5	
	23/10/18		work continued on Railway Embankment F 29 a 0.5. Roads repaired & cleared LE MOLINEL & LE NOIR BONNET	EW
	24/10/18		work commenced on removing demolished Iron Girder Bridge at F 27 b 9.9 at 5 am several charges of Gun Cotton were placed on fallen structure so that it could be removed from Canal Bed. Derricks were rigged on Banks of canal & work of clearing was in progress	EW
			Repairs to Road alongside Canal de Roubaix from PLOMEUX Lock to COTTIGNY LOCK.	

D. D. & L., London, E.C.
(A10266) Wt W5300/P713 750,000 2/18 Sch. 52 Forms/C2118/16

Instructions regarding War Diaries and Intelligence Summaries are contained in F. S. Regs., Part II. and the Staff Manual respectively. Title pages will be prepared in manuscript.

WAR DIARY

or

~~INTELLIGENCE SUMMARY.~~

(Erase heading not required.) H.Q. 40th Divl. Engineers

Army Form C. 2118.

Place	Date	Hour	Summary of Events and Information	Remarks and references to Appendices
MOUVAUX	25/10/18		CRE 40th Div met CRE 31st Div to arrange for taking over work 1 Section 229th Field Coy moved in advance to MECHIN & one Section 231st Field Co RE to LEERS NORD	EW
	26/10/18		229th Field Coy RE moved to NECHIN Sheet 37/H 14 c 6.8 231st " " " Sheet 37/H 8 Central	EW
			Bridging Equipment was sent forward to NECHIN & a large amount of Timber was conveyed from WAMBRECHIES to H 10 a in readiness for throwing Bridges over L'ESCAUT RIVER Weekly Strength 1 off. 6 or. attached 2 off. 10 or.	EW
LANNOY	27/10/18		CRE Head Quarters removed to 24 RUE DE LILLE LANNOY Sheet 37 G 15 d 2.8 224th Field Coy moved to Sheet 37 G 5 c 0.0.	EW
	28/10/18		CRE & GOC 121 Bde made a reconnaissance of L'ESCAUT RIVER at dawn A Footbridge was placed over the River L'ESCAUT at PECQ by the 229th Field Coy RE completed at 19.30 hrs an attempt to throw a Bridge over the River L'ESCAUT by the 231st Field Co was unsuccessful owing to shell fire & enemy machine gun fire	EW
	29.10.18		Routine	EW
	30.10.18		231st Field Coy RE succeeded in placing a footbridge over L'ESCAUT River at WARCOING C 20 c 7.5	EW
	31.10.18		231st Field Coy RE placed another footbridge over the L'ESCAULT River WARCOING C 20 d 7.9 Bridge completed by 224th Field Coy RE over CANAL DE ROUBAIX A 27 d 1.9 Sheet 37. axle load 6 tons span 17'-0" made with salved R.S.Js. 7" x 3¼"	EW

D. D. & L., London, E.C.
(A10266) Wt W5300/P713 750,000 2/16 Sch. 52 Forms/C2118/16

Army Form C. 2118.

WAR DIARY
or
INTELLIGENCE SUMMARY.

(Erase heading not required.)

Instructions regarding War Diaries and Intelligence Summaries are contained in F. S. Regs., Part II. and the Staff Manual respectively. Title pages will be prepared in manuscript.

Place	Date	Hour	Summary of Events and Information	Remarks and references to Appendices
BRIDGE AT D.24.d.1.7. SHEET 36				

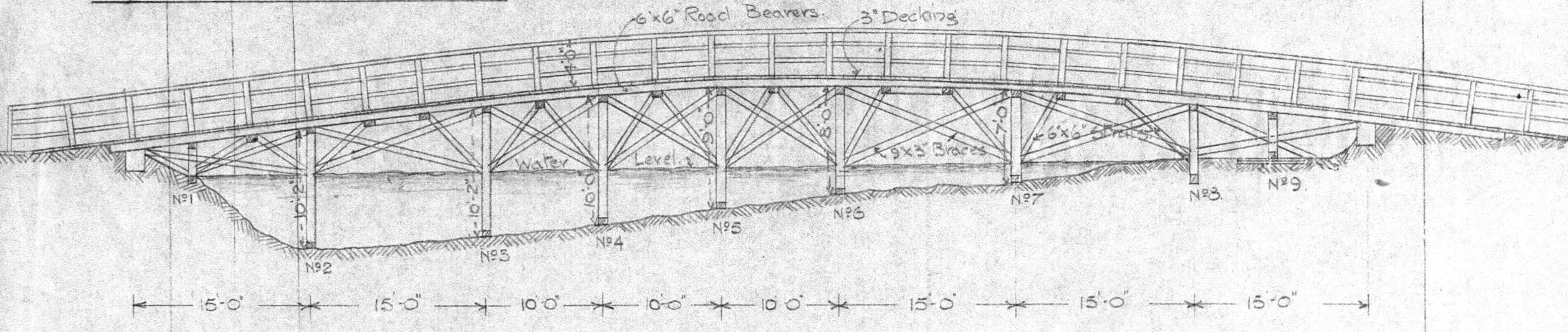

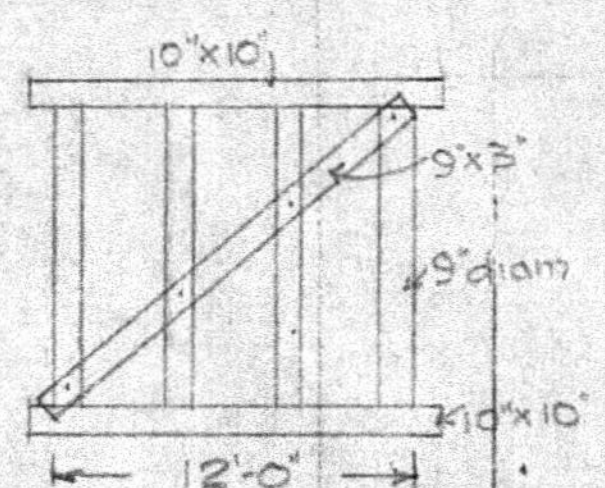

No4 TRESTLE.

D. D. & L., London, E.C.
(A10266) Wt W5300/P713 750,000 2/16 Sch. 52 Forms/C2118/16

Instructions regarding War Diaries and Intelligence Summaries are contained in F. S. Regs., Part II. and the Staff Manual respectively. Title pages will be prepared in manuscript.

WAR DIARY
or
INTELLIGENCE SUMMARY.

H.Q. 40th (*Erase heading not required.*) Div'l Engineers

Army Form C. 2118.

Place	Date	Hour	Summary of Events and Information	Remarks and references to Appendices

BRIDGE OVER CANAL of ROUBAIX. F.27.b.9.9. SHEET 36.

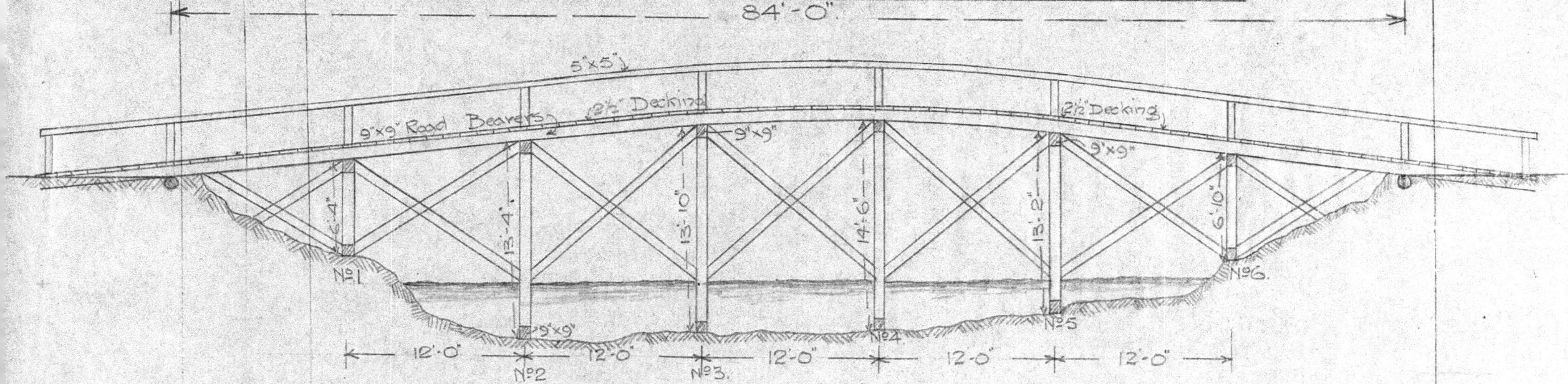

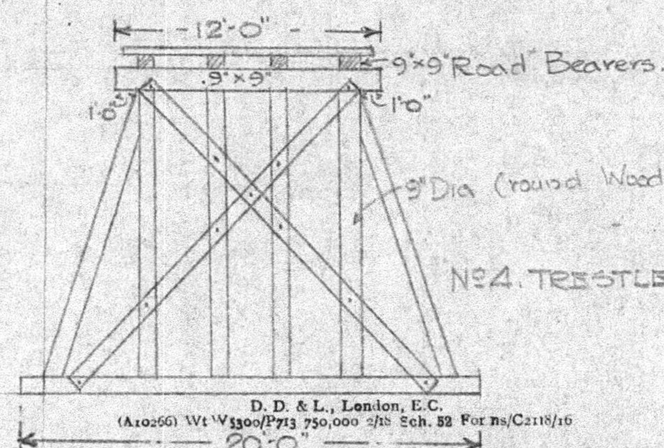

No4. TRESTLE.

D. D. & L., London, E.C.
(A10266) Wt W5300/P713 750,000 2/18 Sch. 52 Forms/C2118/16

Instructions regarding War Diaries and Intelligence Summaries are contained in F. S. Regs., Part II. and the Staff Manual respectively. Title pages will be prepared in manuscript.

WAR DIARY
or
INTELLIGENCE SUMMARY.
(Erase heading not required.)

Army Form C. 2118.

Place	Date	Hour	Summary of Events and Information	Remarks and references to Appendices

BRIDGE AT COTTIGNY LOCK. L.2.d.40.55. SHEET 36.

for Infantry in Fours only.

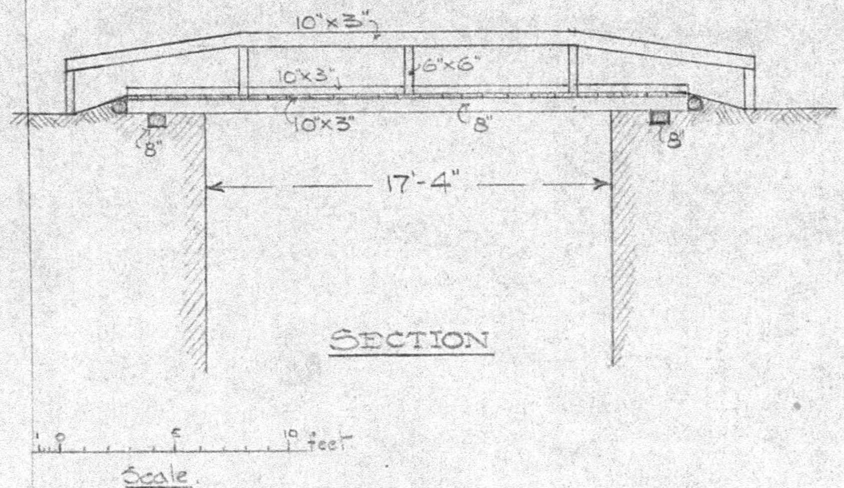

SECTION

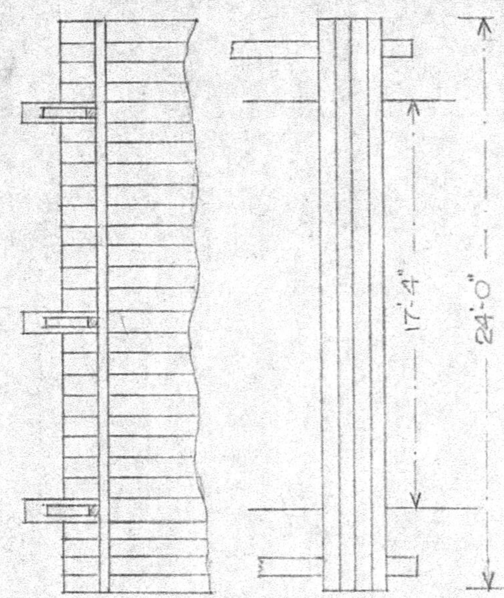

PLAN

Roadbearers . 24' ROUND
Roadbearers @ 5'-6" centres.
Between Ribands 7'-6"
Chesses 12'-0". 3. 15'-0" to take
handrail struts.

D. D. & L., London, E.C.
(A10266) Wt W3300/P713 750,000 2/18 Sch. 52 Forms/C2118/16

Army Form C. 2118.

WAR DIARY
or
INTELLIGENCE SUMMARY.
(Erase heading not required.)

Instructions regarding War Diaries and Intelligence Summaries are contained in F. S. Regs., Part II. and the Staff Manual respectively. Title pages will be prepared in manuscript.

Place	Date	Hour	Summary of Events and Information	Remarks and references to Appendices
			BRIDGE AT L.8.a.5.2. SHEET 36.	

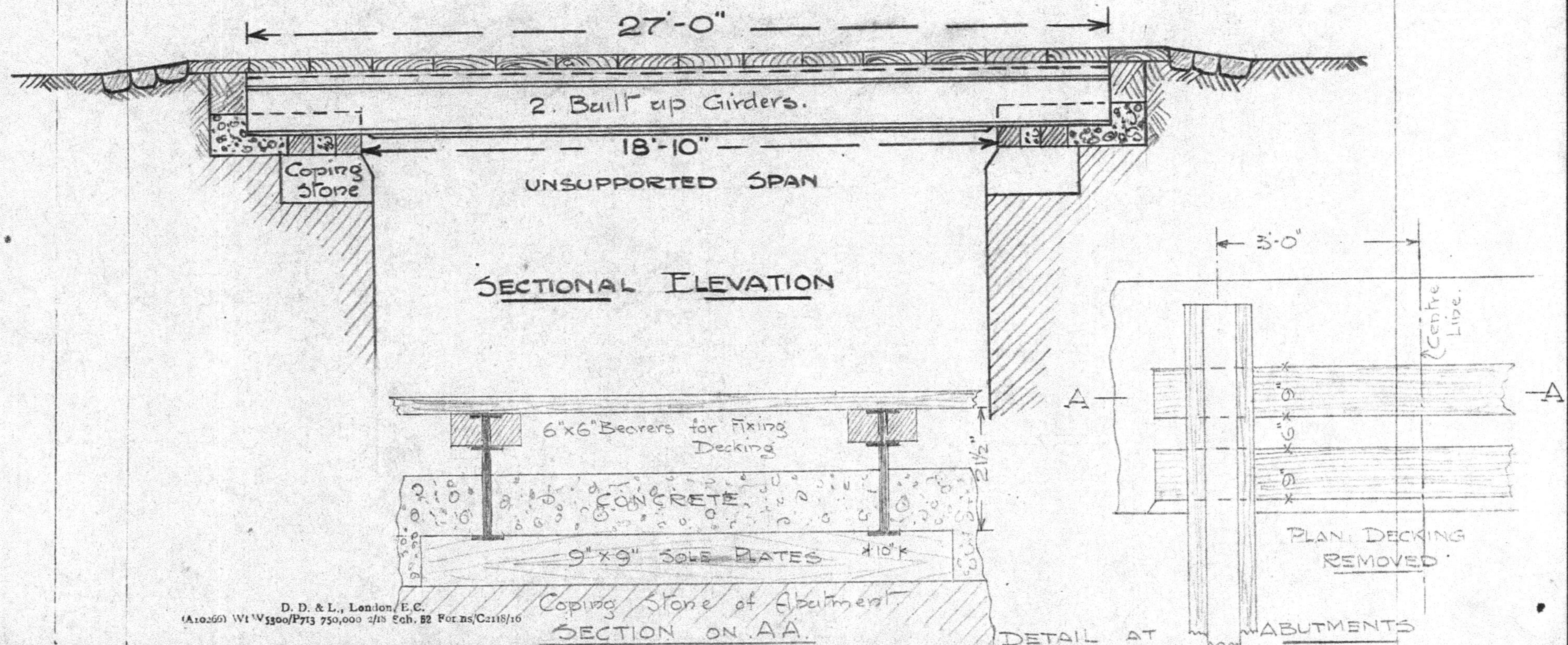

D. D. & L., London, E.C.
(A10266) Wt W5300/P713 750,000 2/18 Sch. 52 Forms/C2118/16

Army Form C. 2118.

WAR DIARY

or

INTELLIGENCE SUMMARY.

H.Q. 40th (*Erase heading not required.*) Div. Engineers

Instructions regarding War Diaries and Intelligence Summaries are contained in F. S. Regs., Part II. and the Staff Manual respectively. Title pages will be prepared in manuscript.

Place	Date	Hour	Summary of Events and Information	Remarks, and references to Appendices
			TEMPORARY BRIDGE OVER RIVER AT E.26.d.50.37. Sheet 36.	

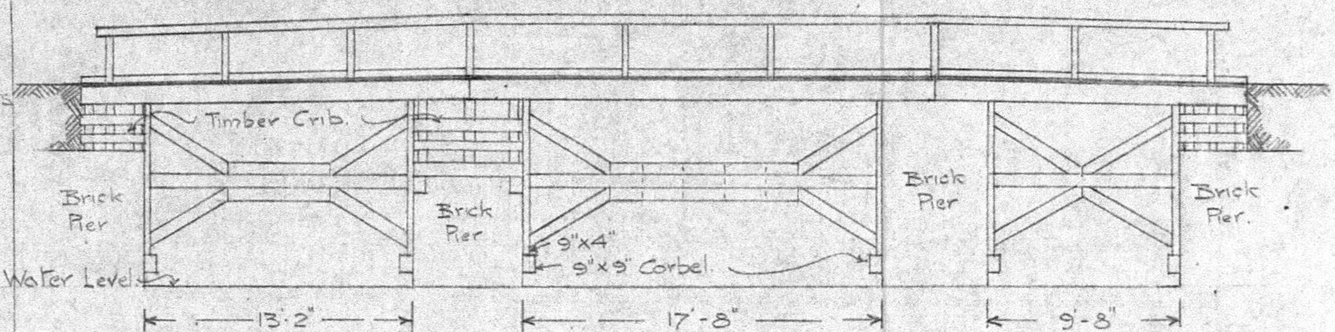

Note: 8 - 9½" x 9½" road bearers in each end bay
9 - 9½" x 9½" in centre bay

Approx. Scale 8ft = 1 inch.

D. D. & L., London, E.C.
(A10266) Wt W3300/P713 750,000 2/15 Sch. 52 Forms/C2118/16

To C. R. E.
40th Division

1 - 10cm Gun received
with thanks.

J. H. Parker
2/Lieut
for Lieut Colonel
General Staff 40th Division

14/11/18.

Instructions regarding War Diaries and Intelligence Summaries are contained in F. S. Regs., Part II. and the Staff Manual respectively. Title pages will be prepared in manuscript.

Army Form C. 2118.

WAR DIARY
or
~~INTELLIGENCE SUMMARY.~~
(Erase heading not required.)

H Q 40th Div Engineers

Place	Date	Hour	Summary of Events and Information	Remarks and references to Appendices
LANNOY	1/11/18		Routine	EW
	2/11/18		231st Field Coy R E completed a footbridge over L'ESCAUT RIVER at C 15 central Strength 2 off 9 or attached 2 off 12 or	EW
	3/11/18		Routine	EW
	4/11/18		Routine	EW
	5/11/18		Routine	EW
	6/11/18		It being reported that the enemy was about to retire from the L'Escaut another footbridge was thought necessary to facilitate the crossing for our Infantry. 229th Field Coy threw a flying Bridge over the river at 37/I 2.c 85 30 during the night & completed same by 0315 hrs	EW
	7/11/18		Routine	EW
	8/11/18		2 Barrel Pier Bridges were made & placed across River L'Escaut at WARCOING to replace two German float Bridges which had become unuseable. The work was carried out by 231st Field Coy on the night 8/9th Nov. 229th Field Coy also built a Bridge for Infantry in File on the old steel Girders of Bridge at PECQ	EW
	9/11/18		The Enemy having retired during the night 229th Field Coy commenced work on a Pontoon Bridge at PECQ & 231st Field Coy on a Bridge to take Pack Mules at WARCOING The Bridge at WARCOING was completed at 1700 hrs & The Bridge at PECQ was ready for Horse Transport at 19.30 hrs. Strength 2 off 9 or attached 2 off 10 or	EW

D. D. & L., London, E.C.
(A10266) Wt W5300/P713 750,000 2/13 Sch. 52 Forms/C2118/16

Instructions regarding War Diaries and Intelligence Summaries are contained in F. S. Regs., Part II. and the Staff Manual respectively. Title pages will be prepared in manuscript.

Army Form C. 2118.

WAR DIARY
or
~~INTELLIGENCE SUMMARY.~~
(Erase heading not required.)

HQ 40th Div'l Engineers

Place	Date	Hour	Summary of Events and Information	Remarks and references to Appendices
LANNOY	10/11/18		231st Field Coy RE commenced the erection of a Timber Trestle Bridge over the L'Escaut River at Warcoing to take Motor Lorries	EW
	11/11/18		ARMISTICE SIGNED. Field Coys carried on work as usual. Building Bridge at WARCOING filling craters, repairing demolished culverts, & repairing & cleansing Roads from River L'Escaut to CHEMIN VERT & MOLEMBAIX	EW
	12/11/18		Routine	EW
	13/11/18		Bridge over River L'Escaut completed in 36 working hours (by day only). The depth of the River was 12ft with a very strong current which made it very difficult to place the Trestles in position. Detail drawing of this Bridge is attached	EW
	14/11/18		CRE attended a Conference held by the Corps Commander to discuss the Army Educational Scheme. A German Field Gun taken at D 27. c 8 3. was removed from Gun Pit to PLACE CARNOT in LANNOY & receipt obtained for same from 40th Div General Staff	EW EW
	15/11/18		229th Field Coy moved to LE MOLINEL 36/F 25c & 231st Field Coy were transferred for work under CRE XVth Corps Troops moved to LA MADELINE. 36/K21 c 3.3.	EW
	16/11/18		Routine Strength 1 off 8 or. attached 2 off 10 or	EW

D. D. & L., London, E.C.
(A10266) Wt W3300/P713 750,000 2/18 Sch. 52 Forms/C2118/16

Army Form C. 2118.

WAR DIARY
or
~~INTELLIGENCE SUMMARY.~~
(Erase heading not required.) H.Q. 40th Divl. Engineers

Instructions regarding War Diaries and Intelligence Summaries are contained in F. S. Regs., Part II. and the Staff Manual respectively. Title pages will be prepared in manuscript.

Place	Date	Hour	Summary of Events and Information	Remarks and references to Appendices
LANNOY	17/11/18		Detachments of Field Coys & Signal Coy attended a Thanksgiving Service at ROUBAIX of the 2nd Army & took part in the march past the Army Commander	EW
	18/11/18		Routine	EW
	19/11/18		CRE visited the Bourgmestres of Warcoing & Herrines to arrange for REs to assist in making these villages habitable	EW
	20/11/18		Routine	EW
	21/11/18		Routine	EW
	22/11/18		Routine	EW
	23/11/18		Routine Strength 1 off 8 or attached 3 off 11 or	EW
	24/11/18		Routine	EW
ROUBAIX	25/11/18		H Q Division moved to ROUBAIX. CRE's H.Q. at No 4 RUE DES ARTS ROUBAIX	EW
	26/11/18		Routine	EW
	27/11/18		CRE proceeded on Leave to Paris & Major F W Clark MC RE O/c 229th Field Coy RE assumed command of the 40th Divl Engineers	EW
	28/11/18		Routine	EW

D. D. & L., London, E.C.
(A10266) Wt W3300/P713 750,000 2/18 Sch. 52 Forms/C2118/16

Instructions regarding War Diaries and Intelligence Summaries are contained in F. S. Regs., Part II. and the Staff Manual respectively. Title pages will be prepared in manuscript.

WAR DIARY
or
INTELLIGENCE SUMMARY.

Army Form C. 2118.

40th Div. ~~(Erase heading not required.)~~ Engineers

Place	Date	Hour	Summary of Events and Information	Remarks and references to Appendices
ROUBAIX	29/11/18		a/CRE attended Conference of CREs at Corps respecting Corps scheme of Technical Education	EW
	30/11/18		Routine Strength 1 off 8 or attached 3 off 10 or.	EW

D. D. & L., London, E.C.
(A10266) Wt W5300/P713 750,000 2/18 Sch. 52 Forms/C2118/16

Instructions regarding War Diaries and Intelligence Summaries are contained in F. S. Regs., Part II. and the Staff Manual respectively. Title pages will be prepared in manuscript.

WAR DIARY
or
INTELLIGENCE SUMMARY.
(Erase heading not required.)

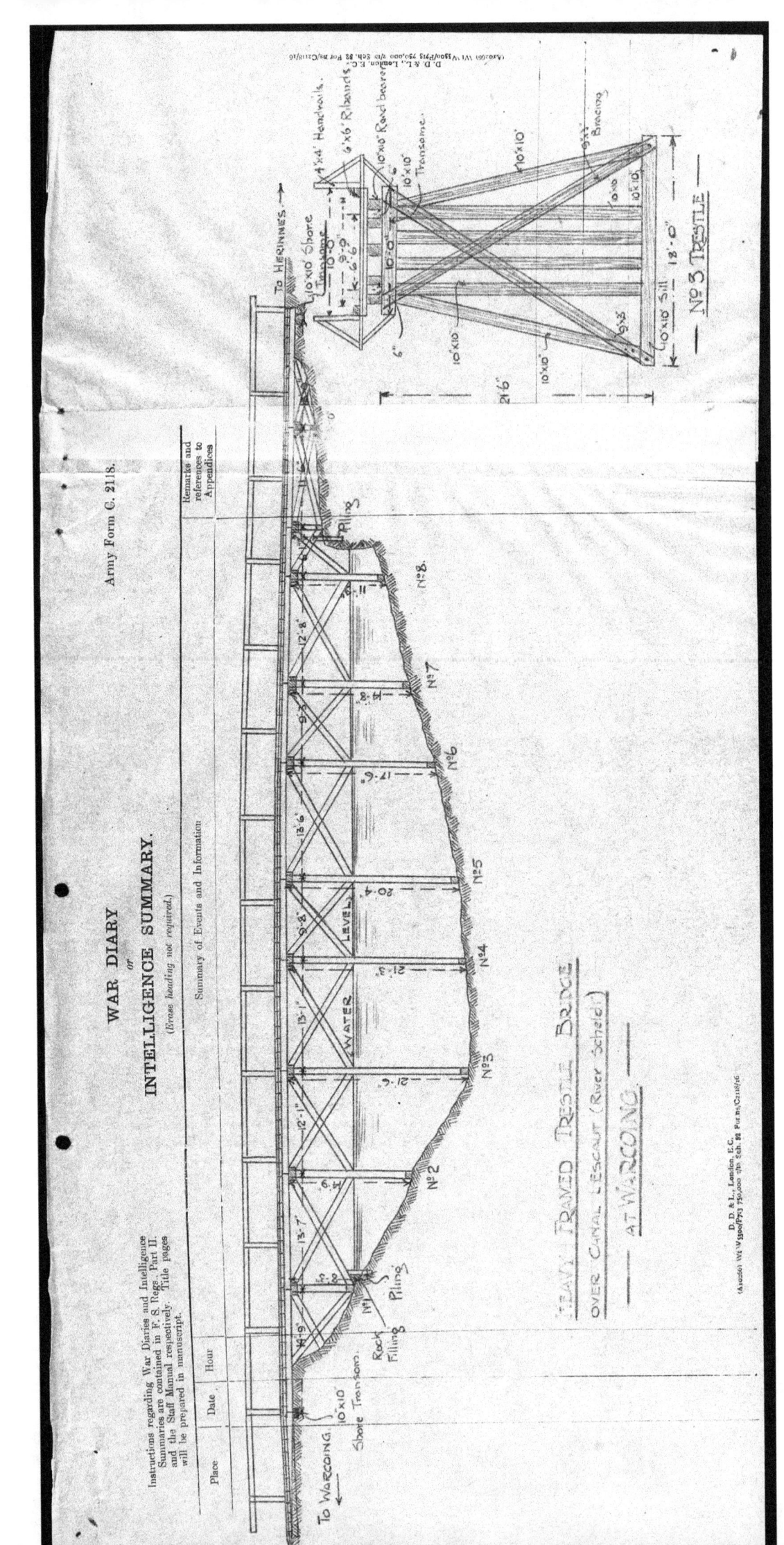

Army Form C. 2118.

Place	Date	Hour	Summary of Events and Information	Remarks and references to Appendices

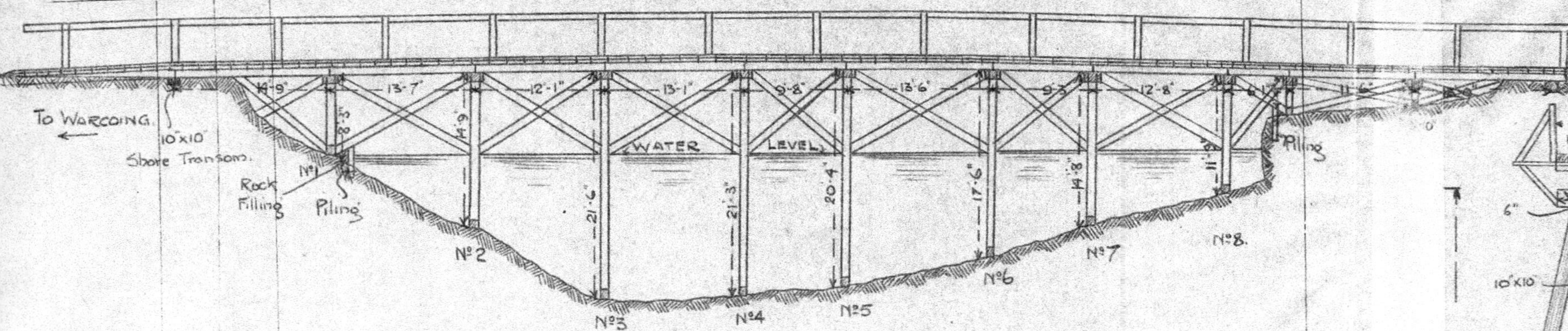

HEAVY FRAMED TRESTLE BRIDGE
OVER CANAL L'ESCAUT (River Scheldt)
AT WARCOING

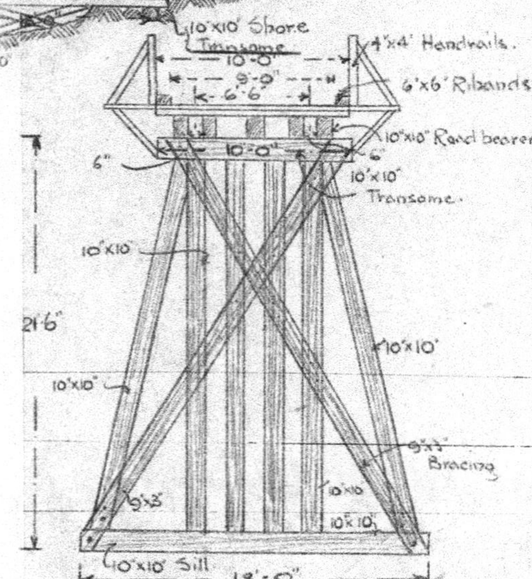

— Nº 3 TRESTLE —

D. D. & L., London, E.C.
(A10260) Wt W5300/P713 750,000 2/15 Sch. 52 Forms/C2118/16

Army Form C. 2118.

WAR DIARY
or
~~INTELLIGENCE SUMMARY.~~

HQ 40th (~~Erase heading not required.~~) Dvl Engineers

Instructions regarding War Diaries and Intelligence Summaries are contained in F. S. Regs., Part II. and the Staff Manual respectively. Title pages will be prepared in manuscript.

Place	Date	Hour	Summary of Events and Information	Remarks and references to Appendices
ROUBAIX	1/12/18		Routine	EW
	2/12/18		Routine First Class assembled at the RE Instructional Workshops which have been instituted at Wambrechies Dump as Refresher Courses for men who previous to the war were employed in the following trades for which classes have been arranged Carpenters Joiners Tinsmiths Blacksmiths Bricklayers Wheelwrights & Plumbers. A Comdt, Adjutant & staff has been formed of RE Officers & NCOs. Students are detailed from Infantry Battalions & Dvl Troops. 224th Field Coy RE moved to BAISIEUX 37/M17d7.6 for work under CE XVth Corps	EW
	3/12/18		Routine	EW
	4/12/18		Routine	EW
	5/12/18		CRE returned from leave to Paris	EW
	6/12/18		Routine	EW
	7/12/18		Routine - Strength - 2 Officers 6 O.R. Attached 1 Officer and 10 O.R.	EW
	8/12/18		Routine CRE inspected Billets Recreation & School Rooms of 231st Field Coy RE	EW
	9/12/18		Routine CRE visited GOC 120th Inf. Bgde. GOC 121st Inf. Bdge & 17 Bn Worcester Regt Pioneers	EW

D. D. & L., London, E.C.
(A10266) Wt W5300/P713 750,000 2/18 Sch. 52 Forms/C2118/16

Army Form C. 2118.

WAR DIARY
or
~~INTELLIGENCE SUMMARY.~~
40th Dvl (~~Erase heading not required.~~) Engineers

Instructions regarding War Diaries and Intelligence Summaries are contained in F. S. Regs., Part II. and the Staff Manual respectively. Title pages will be prepared in manuscript.

Place	Date	Hour	Summary of Events and Information	Remarks and references to Appendices
ROUBAIX	10/12/18		CRE made a tour of inspection of R.E. School of Instruction at Wambrechies	H.G. H.G.
	11/12/18		Routine	H.G.
	12/12/18		Routine	
	13/12/18		attended CEs conference of CREs on Education Scheme & reported on progress made with RE School of Instruction at Wambrechies	H.G.
	14/12/18		Routine Strength 2 officers 7 O.R. Attached - 1 officer 9 O.R.	H.G.
	15/12/18		CRE visited 224th Field Coy at BAISIEUX & inspected work on P.O.W Camp BAISIEUX	H.G.
	16/12/18		Routine.	H.G.
	17.12.18		Adjutant proceeded to U.K. with Draft of Coalminers for demobilization	H.G.
	18.12.18		Routine	H.G.
	19.12.18		CRE attended G.O.C. Conference on Educational Schemes &c - Routine	H.G.
	20.12.18		Routine.	H.G.
	21.12.18		Routine. - 1 officer 5 O.R. Attached 1 officer 12 O.R.	H.G.
	22.12.18		Routine	H.G.
	23.12.18		40th Signal Coy. paraded for inspection by Divisional Commander. - CRE was unable to attend owing to illness. G.O.C. did not arrive at Parade Ground, and parade was dismissed without being inspected. Routine.	H.G.

D. D. & L., London, E.C.
(A10266) Wt W5300/P713 750,000 8/15 Sch. 52 Forms/C2118/16

Army Form C. 2118.

WAR DIARY

~~or~~

~~INTELLIGENCE SUMMARY.~~

- H.Q. 40th Divl. ~~(Erase heading not required.)~~ Engineers -

Instructions regarding War Diaries and Intelligence Summaries are contained in F. S. Regs., Part II. and the Staff Manual respectively. Title pages will be prepared in manuscript.

Place	Date	Hour	Summary of Events and Information	Remarks and references to Appendices
ROUBAIX.	24.12.18.		C.R.E. met Coy Commanders at his H.Q. and discussed matters connected with Demobilization and Reconstruction of R.E. at	H.L.
	25.12.18.		Office closed, except for urgent business. C.R.E. visited Sig. Coy and 231st Field Coy R.E. Unable to visit the other Coys owing to breakdown of car.	H.L.
	26.12.18		Routine.	H.L.
	27.12.18		Routine.	H.L.
	28.12.18		Routine - C.R.E. visited R.E. School of Instruction, Wambrechies. Strength 1 Officer 5 O.R. Attached 1 Officer 10 O.R.	H.L.
	29.12.18		Routine	H.L.
	30.12.18		Routine	H.L.
	31.12.18		Routine.	

D. D. & L., London, E.C.
(A10266) Wt W5300/P713 750,000 2/18 Sch. 52 Forms/C2118/16

Army Form C. 2118.

WAR DIARY
or
~~INTELLIGENCE SUMMARY~~.
40th ~~Divisional~~ ~~(Erase heading not required.)~~ / Engineers.

Instructions regarding War Diaries and Intelligence Summaries are contained in F. S. Regs., Part II., and the Staff Manual respectively. Title pages will be prepared in manuscript.

Place	Date	Hour	Summary of Events and Information	Remarks and references to Appendices
	1919.			
ROUBAIX.	1.1.19.		Routine.	H.G.
	2.1.19.		C.R.E. proceeded on leave to U.K. O.C. 224th Field Coy R.E. (Major Hunter [illegible]) took over duties of C.R.E.	H.G.
	3.1.19		Routine.	H.G.
	4.1.19		C.R.E. visited R.E. School of Instruction, Wambrechies. G.O.C. 120th and 121st Infantry Brigades. Strength 6 O.R. Attached 2 officers 10 O.R.	H.G. H.G.
	5.1.19.		Routine.	H.G.
	6.1.19.		Routine	
	7.1.19 – 16		Routine. Strength 11/1/19 6 O.R. Attached 1 off 10 O.R.	H.G.
	17.1.19		C.R.E. attended Corps Conference on R.E. Memorial and various subjects	[illegible]
	18-21.		Routine. Strength 18/1/19 5 O.R. Attached 1 off 0 O.R.	
	22.1.19		Lt Col. Walsan [?] D.S.O. R.E. (C.R.E.) returned to Division under orders from W.O. to hand over, preparatory to leaving for duty in VLADIVOSTOCK.	[illegible]

D. D. & L., London, E.C.
(A10266) Wt W5300/P713 750,000 2/18 Sch. 52 Forms/C2118/16

Instructions regarding War Diaries and Intelligence Summaries are contained in F. S. Regs., Part II. and the Staff Manual respectively. Title pages will be prepared in manuscript.

WAR DIARY
or
INTELLIGENCE SUMMARY.
(Erase heading not required.)

Army Form C. 2118.

Place	Date	Hour	Summary of Events and Information	Remarks and references to Appendices
ROUBAIX	1919			
	23-24		Routine.	
	25/1.		do. Strength 1 off 5 O.R. Attached 1 off 7 O.R.	
	26/1.		2/Lieut Godwin rejoined from leave to U.K. and assumed duties as Adjutant 40th Divisional Engineers.	F.E.G.
	27/1.		Routine. C.E. XV. Corps visited C.R.E. and discussed work in hand in connection with Bridge to be erected at ROUBAIX – Lt Col. Wilson handed over duties to Major E. L. Martin M.C. R.E.	F.E.G.
	28/1.		Lt Col Wilson M.C. departed for W.O. – Lt Col. F.G. Hyland M.C. R.E. took over Office of C.R.E. 40th Division from Major Martin M.C. R.E. Lt Col. Hyland M.C. (C.R.E.) visited R.E. School, Wambrechies and 229th Field Coy R.E.	F.E.G.
	29/1.		Routine – C.R.E. visited G.O.C. 119th Infy Brigade, and 224th Field Coy R.E.	F.E.G.
	30/1.		C.R.E. visited Bridge at ROUBAIX in course of erection by 231st Field Coy R.E.	F.E.G.
	31/1.		C.R.E. attended Corps Conference at C.E. XV Corps H.Q.	F.E.G.

D. D. & L., London, E.C.
(A10266) Wt W5300/P713 750,000 2/18 Sch. 52 Forms/C2118/16

Instructions regarding War Diaries and Intelligence Summaries are contained in F. S. Regs., Part II. and the Staff Manual respectively. Title pages will be prepared in manuscript.

WAR DIARY

~~or~~

~~INTELLIGENCE SUMMARY.~~

~~(Erase heading not required.)~~

Army Form C. 2118.

— 40th Divisional Engineers —

Place	Date	Hour	Summary of Events and Information	Remarks and references to Appendices
	1919			
ROUBAIX.	Febry. 1.		Routine. State. 1 Off. 5 O.R. attached 2 Off. 8 O.R.	H.G.
	2		Routine	H.G.
	3		Routine	H.G.
	4		Routine.	H.G.
	6.		Routine. - O.C. 229 Field Coy. (Major Clark M.C.) proceeded to England for demobilization - Lieut Rolfe	H.G.
	7		229th Field Coy. R.E. move from LE MOLINEL to CROIX 36/L7 B03. - Lieut Power R.E. 224 Field Coy. R.E. appointed Adjt. vice - Captain E. Walker demobilised.	H.G.
	8.		Routine. State 1 Off. 5 O.R. attached 1 Off. 7 O.R.	H.G.
	9.		Routine	H.G.
	10		Routine.	H.G.
	11		Routine.	H.G.
	12.		Routine - R.E. School of Instruction WAMBRECHIES closed.	H.G.
	13		Routine - Instructions received from H.Q. 40 Division to hold 231 Field Coy. in readiness for Army of Occupation (Rhine).	H.G.
	14		Routine	H.G.
	15.		Routine State, 1 Off. 3 O.R. attached 1 Off. 5 O.R.	H.G.
	16		Routine	H.G.
	17		Routine. - Bridge at 36/F23 central launched.	H.G.
	18		Routine	H.G.
	19		Routine	H.G.
	20		Routine	H.G.

D. D. & L., London, E.C.
(A10266) Wt W5300/P713 750,000 2/18 Sch. 52 Forms/C2118/16

Instructions regarding War Diaries and Intelligence Summaries are contained in F. S. Regs., Part II. and the Staff Manual respectively. Title pages will be prepared in manuscript.

WAR DIARY
or
INTELLIGENCE SUMMARY.
(Erase heading not required.)

Army Form C. 2118.

Place	Date	Hour	Summary of Events and Information	Remarks and references to Appendices
Roubaix	21.2.19		Routine	HL
	22.2.19		Routine Sick 1 off 2 OR attached 1 off 5 OR	HL
	23.2.19		Routine	HL
	24.2.19		Routine	HL
	25.2.19		Routine	HL
	26.2.19		Routine	HL
	27.2.19		Routine	HL
	28.2.19		Routine. C.R.E. (Lt Col. Hyland) proceeded to U.K. on Special leave (14 days) and Capt. J.G. Vice, (229 Field Coy. R.E.) took over duties of C.R.E.	HL

D. D. & L., London, E.C.
(A10266) Wt W5300/P713 750,000 2/18 Sch. 52 Forms/C2118/16

www.ingramcontent.com/pod-product-compliance
Lightning Source LLC
Chambersburg PA
CBHW081538160426
43191CB00011B/1787
* 9 7 8 1 4 7 4 5 1 9 3 1 1 *